French Napoleonic
Line Infantry

1796–1815

Emir Bukhari

ALMARK PUBLISHING CO. LTD., LONDON

First Published – November 1973

ISBN 0 85524 153 5 (hard cover edition)
ISBN 0 85524 154 3 (paper covered edition)

Printed in Great Britain by
Byron Press Ltd., 59 Palmerston Road, Wealdstone, Middlesex
for the publishers, Almark Publishing Co. Ltd.,
49 Malden Way, New Malden, Surrey KT3 6EA, England

Introduction

This work is intended to serve as a handy reference guide to the uniforms and equipment of infantry regiments, presenting at once both the official decrees as to organization and dress and the often far-removed actuality found in the field.

To facilitate this, numerous full page illustrations are included throughout with clear colouring detail to enable the reader to find quickly and easily the appropriate reference he seeks. To avoid unnecessary repetition the colours of waistcoats, breeches and gaiters were all off-white, the webbing white and boots black. This is correct for all regiments unless indicated otherwise. The musket had natural wood 'furniture' and white metal fittings, excepting for élite companies where they were generally copper coloured. The musket sling was pipe-clayed white and had a copper buckle. Buttons were copper, unless specified otherwise, and bore the regimental number.

My special thanks are due to Gerry Embleton without whose knowledge and aid this volume would have been all the poorer. My thanks also to Miss Sue Armitage for typing the first drafts of this work, and to Mrs. M. Davies for typing the final manuscript.

Thanks are also due to Monsieur Lucien Rousselot without whose arduous research no book on the French Army of the period covered here would be practicable.

E. S. B.

CONTENTS

1: Tactics and Organisation

THE battlefield at Waterloo marked the end of a turbulent and aggressive period in French history. Since 1792 France had been almost continually at war with the rest of Europe and reached its military zenith between the years of 1804 and 1809 under the self-crowned 'Emperor of the French', Napoleon. Through his tactical skill, Spain, Italy, Belgium, Holland, Switzerland, Austria, Prussia, Denmark and innumerable German states became satellites of France. This book is about the men who marched from Torres Vedras to Moscow, Albuera to Waterloo, Napoleon's Infantry.

By 1805, war was no longer for the professionals and zealous volunteers; the Directory Decree of the 8th Fructidor, Year VIII, extending that of February 14, 1793, made by the defunct Convention, proclaimed all bachelors between the ages of 20 and 25 liable for military service. This period had no time limit during wartime, and thus, a conscript called to the colours at Boulogne in 1805, unless subsequently wounded, maimed, lost, diseased, or killed, would find himself on the field of Waterloo, ten years later.

From 50,000 men per year under the Consulate, the ranks were swelled by 160,000 per year by 1808, and by 1812 no less than 280,000 callow youths were despatched to training camps every year. Substitutes could, in the early years, be purchased for 2 to 4,000 francs; by 1813 the premium had inflated to 12,000 francs. It is also interesting to note that, from the beginning of hostilities in 1805, marriages had increased by 50 per cent by 1809.

Having been conscripted the first step in turning them into soldiers was their instruction by NCOs, veterans of the Revolutionary and more recent wars, in the precise drill of Napoleonic infantry. Dressed in their white fatigue uniforms, they would be made to march and counter-march the area of the parade-ground, mock muskets against their left shoulders, to a rigid 76 paces a minute for four hours a day. Musket training would fill the rest of their working day, loading and re-loading in the rigid twelve movements per minute. Live ammunition was distributed twice a week, more in the interest of getting the men used to the noise of their weapons than of improving their markmanship. Finally, every Sunday a complete revue would be held, the troops being allowed to don their full dress blue coats, bicorns and gaiters.

Thus accoutred, they would perform their manoeuvres under the eyes of their colonels and senior officers rather than the NCOs who drilled them throughout the week.

One can scarcely imagine a Napoleonic battlefield without rank upon rank of troops, shoulder to shoulder, all of them moving and firing in one general direction. The reason for this is apparent when one realises that the infantryman was armed with a smooth-bore musket which in relative terms was no great advance on the long-bow as a means of killing the enemy.

The French infantry musket of the Napoleonic period dated back to 1777, was in service until 1809, and was then slowly replaced by a slightly modified version, the Year IX model. It was 1.53 metres long, with a 40.6 cm long detachable bayonet; thus, the effective length when assaulting an enemy was 1.936 metres, or, approximately 6 foot 3½ inches. It's weight was 4.65 kilograms (10 lbs 4 oz). Calibres varied considerably, but averaged 1.75 cm.

As we have seen, loading this weapon took an exhaustive minute of twelve co-ordinated movements. Essentially the method was to remove from the leather cartridge pouch on the right hip, one of the fifty cartridges kept therein, tear off the tip with one's teeth, empty the majority of the powder down the barrel (a hazardous business this, if the bayonet was affixed), wad it down tightly with the ramrod, spit the ball retained in one's mouth down on top of it, ram that down firmly too, then, finally, empty the remaining powder on to the flashpan. At the end of this if the powder was the slighest bit damp, the musket would misfire; it was not unusual in the excitement and furore of battle, for the men to ignore this, and go on loading and firing until the weapon blew up as the powder finally ignited.

Another hazard was to leave the ramrod in the barrel, from whence it might, on discharge, possibly impale the enemy but leave the owner without any means of reloading. When the lead ball left the barrel, it had a killing range of 100 to 250 yards, but could still inflict a wound of some kind at up to 1000 yards if aimed high. The odds however, of hitting the selected target at past 100 yards or so were slight. The ball travelled slowly and, being of irregular shape, followed a rather erratic course due to the lack of rifling in the barrel.

To achieve any sort of result with this weapon the only thing to do was to group the men together and have them fire simultaneously and all in the general direction of the target, thus by the law of averages hitting something with effect. Understanding this necessity for large grouping, to have effective firepower, let us now examine the units that each new conscript had to be familiar with and the complex manoeuvres he needed to accomplish as part of those units if he was to survive and carry out his assigned tasks in the heat of an action.

THE COMPANY

The smallest tactical unit of an infantry regiment was the company, formed of anything between 40 and 100 men. Fig 1 depicts company formations.

Fig 1: For maximum firepower the company was deployed in a line or formation. The company is split into two sections ('pelotons'), each three men deep; the first section on the right, the second on the left. This is a sectional view of the company with its face to the top of the page.

The letter placed on individual squares denotes the position of the following persons:

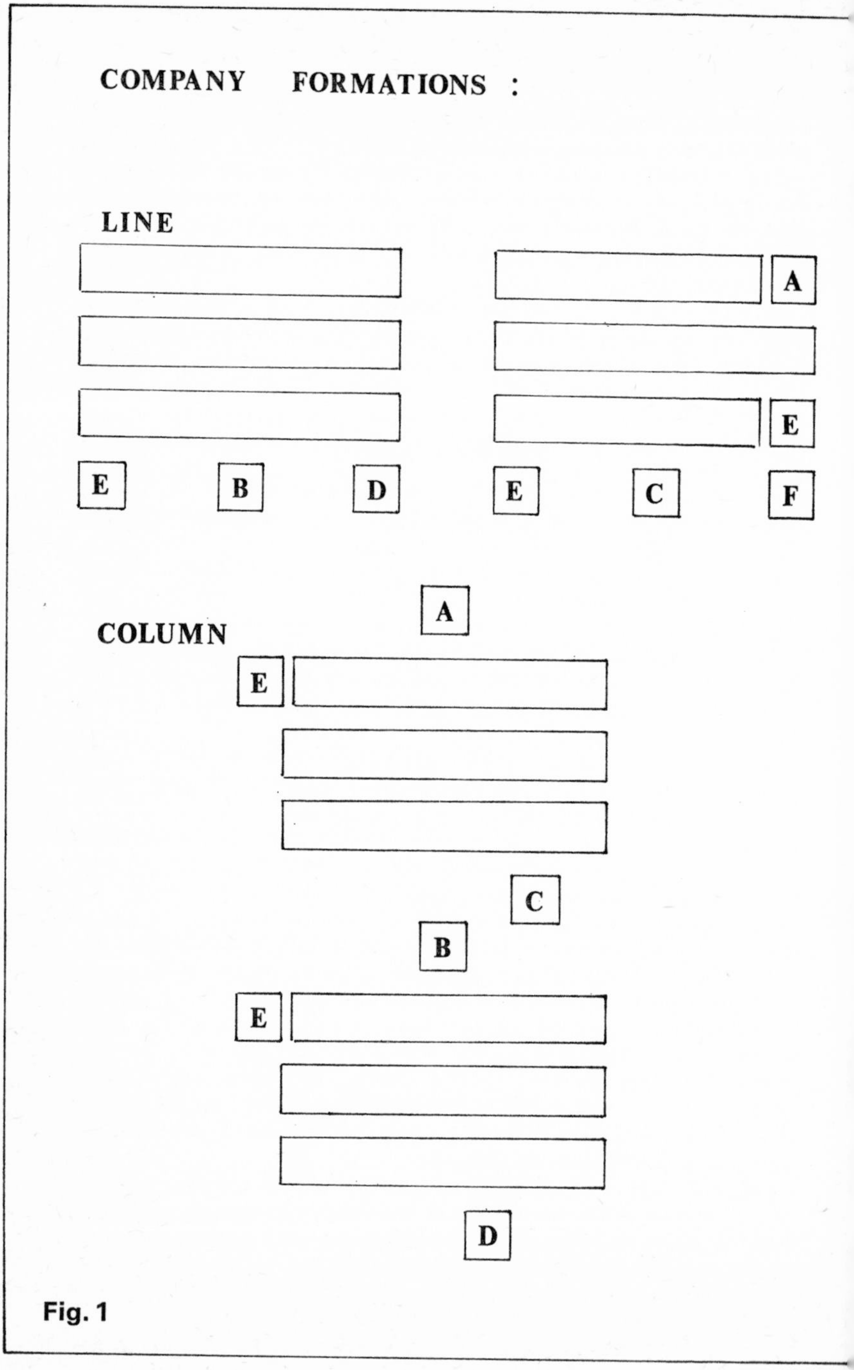

COMPANY FORMATIONS :

LINE

Fig. 1

A. Capitaine (Captain).

B. Lieutenant (1st Lieut).

C. Sous-Lieut. (2nd Lieut).

D. Sergent-Major (Sergeant-Major).

E. Sergent (Sergeant).

F. Sapeur (Sapper).

To form a column of march from this formation, each individual would wheel to the right and form a column of threes.

For an assault, the company would form a 'column by section' with the second peloton following the first. When engaged by another force when on the march they would carry out the reverse of this manoeuvre to form a firing line.

THE DIVISION

This was simply two companies fighting and marching together as a tactical unit; a battalion would be formed of an even number of companies, split into divisions for easier handling.

THE BATTALION

As we can see in Fig 2, the battalion is a conglomerate of three or more divisions (ie, six or more companies). The top illustration shows an assault in 'column by division'.

The Fusilier companies are shown by the numbered boxes, and we note that the companies of each separate division march side by side, not behind each other. We see that at this level, two élite companies are added to the grouping; we shall be dealing with them separately later, for now let us simply note their respective positions: the Voltigeurs (V), newly formed in 1805, take the left flank while the Grenadiers (G) fortify the right.

The benefit of a battalion column such as this was the simplicity with which all these men could be formed into the other formations shown in this illustration.

The line presented the battalion's maximum firepower to the opponent. The Fusiliers again take the centre with the élite companies on each extremity. Fire went from right to left (Grenadiers to Voltigeurs) and thereafter at discretion. The drawback to this deployment is its vulnerability to cavalry attack, owing to its being only three men deep.

To receive cavalry of any type the battalion would form square. The idea being that should any stout horsemen breach the wall of bayonets, they should be trapped within a solid ring of enemy whilst at that very moment the breach was sealed by tightening the side, effectively cutting off their means of escape. The infantry unit in square remained totally intact in theory, the main danger being, for the infantry, that in a line formation it could be split into two parts and in the resulting confusion be sabred piecemeal.

The illustration shows two alternative square formations for a battalion of four divisions. The numbering of the Fusilier companies on the left hand figure show how simple the reforming of a column would be after the cavalry menace had been removed.

The élite companies would pad the shoulders of the square at company strength, as on the left hand figure, or, as on the right, gird the angles at sectional strength. Notice the alternate positioning of these sections.

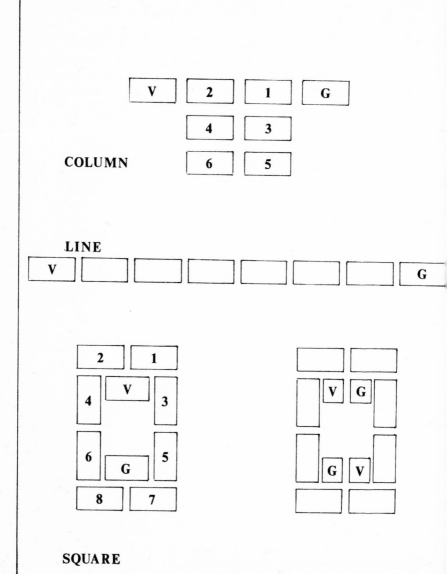

BATTALION FORMATIONS :

Fig. 2

COLUMN

LINE

SQUARE

THE REGIMENT

Two to eight battalions would form a Napoleonic Line Infantry Regiment.

For the assault, each battalion would form itself into the type of column shown at the top of Fig 2. Depending on the type of assault to be delivered and the terrain involved, the battalions could form one behind the other in one immense column, next to one another, or, alternatively, in echelon.

But even the ponderous might of these thousands of men was vulnerable to cavalry attack. In the event, a unit of this size had several alternatives. It could form one gigantic square, up to six men deep per side, as at the Battle of the Pyramids, or, more easily, it could sub-divide into its battalion components, these forming independent squares; in this case the squares would be disposed on the field either in echelon or in a line, with a corner of each square presented to the oncoming foe. Battalion squares were employed at Auerstaedt and Waterloo, though in the latter case it was most notably the 2nd battalion of the 3rd Regiment of Grenadiers of the Guard, who retreated in splendid order of square whilst about them their fellow regiments ran in disorder before the Allied armies. Originally 500 in strength, they were slowly decimated until, finding themselves unable to hold a square formation, they formed small triangles to equal effect. In the end they were all slaughtered because they refused to surrender but this instance highlights the psychological benefit of the square to the infantryman, in so far as he knew that nothing from behind could bowl him over, and that his position was relatively secure as long as he stood his ground.

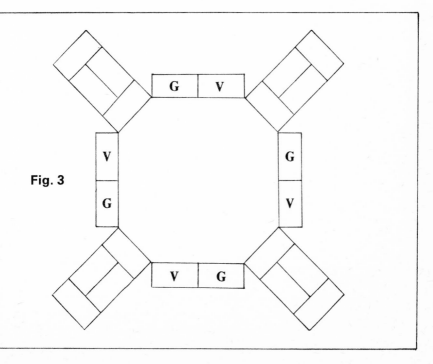

Fig. 3

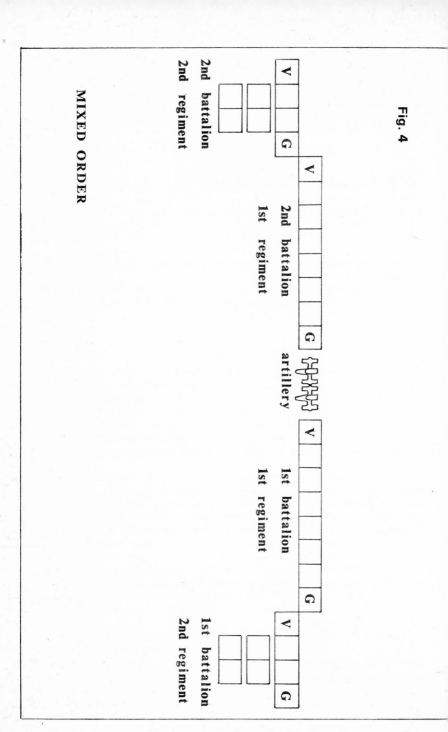

Fig. 4

MIXED ORDER

Fig. 3 shows a most impressive square of four battalions, an arrangement used by the infantry at the Battle of Borodino and later at Weissenfels and Luetzen. In this configuration the Fusilier companies form independent squares that are linked on both sides by élite companies that join them to the others. A quite prodigious amount of firepower was able to be brought into play by this formation and the square provided considerable security.

THE BRIGADE

Two or three regiments formed this tactical unit. The standard assault formation is the subject of Fig 4. The first regiment is deployed in line at the centre presenting fine firepower to the foe, while the second regiment's battalions provide two columns on each extremity. The formation thus provides the benefits of both line firepower and the impact of column assault. In the event of cavalry assailing the units, the two halves of the second regiment would fold back and join together producing a square.

This particular brigade has the luxury of the divisional artillery at its axis. An alternative, and most successful at that, was the placement of a Light Infantry Regiment in this position.

THE DIVISION

There was theoretically, a light infantry regiment for every three line regiments. The addition of such would raise the brigade to the level of Division (not to be confused with 2 companies = 1 Division).

The assault formation of the Division followed closely that shown in Fig 4 excepting that the light regiment would take up the position occupied by the first line regiment. The line regiments would then form regiment strong columns on the extremities, the artillery remaining on the axis.

Finally look again at Fig 4. This deadly formation amalgamates the benefits of both Line firepower and Column assault formation. We can see that should cavalry be presumptious enough to approach, the unit can easily form a virtually unassailable square; the two halves of the 2nd Regiment folding back and meeting behind the artillery.

These then were the essential infantry manoeuvres employed by French infantry regiments between 1804 and 1815. A small change came about from 1813 when the three ranks of the company were reduced to two. One assumes the military tacticians of the day noticed what little detrimental effect the lack of a third row had with British regiments and therefore deleted this wastage of a third of the manpower for the consequent gain in firepower.

Napoleonic infantrymen must have displayed remarkable stoicism for despite shot and shell raining about them, they managed to achieve clock-work precision at the beat of a drum or the sounding of a horn while effecting these formations. It should not be assumed that all of Napoleon's army that was to subjugate Europe in those early years was composed of new recruits. Far from it, approximately 50 per cent were already veterans before he became Emperor . . . but these seasoned warriors were not to last so very long.

2: The Infantry at war

DRILL, endless drill. The recruit, his day starting at 7.30 a.m., was usually unrelieved from the tedious drilling except for soup at 10 a.m. and 4 p.m. He looked towards action as a reprieve from the miseries of routine military life. Many old monasteries and nunneries had been converted to military establishments during the years of the Revolution and in these forbidding corridors many recruits must have reassessed their position as more fitting for criminals than those in whose hands had been laid the pride and safe-keeping of France.

A growing bitterness towards the elusive military administration that thwarted their destinies, denied them their banner at another Arcola, grew and festered until the word at last came. Their chance had finally come . . . Austria and Russia were mobilising! Veterans were quieter.

THE ENDLESS MARCH

The flexibility and speed with which Napoleon's armies achieved their conquests were to cost the infantry arm dearly. Enthusiasm alone does not carry a haversack, weighing between 20 and 30 kilograms, and five kilos of small arms very far. From August 30 to September 25 they marched a total of 700 kilometres, with only three stops lasting 24 hours, at Cambrai, Sedan and Metz. In bedraggled columns of three they staggered, holding one another up, using their muskets for crutches as they reeled the arduous miles away. Many collapsed and were further hurt by the passage of their fellows' boots over them and the blows rained upon their unprotected bodies by the officers' drawn swords. Of the 6,350 men of Friant's Division of Davout's Army Corps, no less than 3,780 were lost en route to Austerlitz. Those who arrived were nearly all boot-less, the footwear issued in Boulogne lasting just about as far as the Rhine. Their feet raw and bleeding, these men, in a state of physical shock and exhaustion, fought Ulm and Austerlitz . . . and won. Napoleon's infantry could evidently take a lot of punishment but this was only the beginning.

Winter firmly set in and the troops were thoughtfully issued with new boots and two spare pairs for their packs, then despatched to pursue the campaign. Torrential rain bucketed down, buffeting their backs as they marched through rivers of mud to their next destination. Grossly underfed, owing to Napoleon's 'live off the land' policy, and exerted beyond endurance, their ranks were depleted further as all year round they marched and counter-marched. December 1806 found them in the treacherous bogs and marshes of Poland. Lewal's Division counted 1,800 men on December 22; it had left 1,650 of these men behind in the deadly countryside by the 28th.

The regiments leaving for Spain after 1807 were to fare no better, for they suffered scorching sand and searing, blistering heat that cracked the skin. There were cases of men staving off thirst by drinking horses' urine, and dysentery was rife.

The suffering continued through to the frozen steppes of Russia where the whole machine all but fell apart. Twenty to forty kilometres a day in all climes they marched, leaving behind a fearful wake of human life to mark their passage.

The roads behind every Army Corps, no matter where it was going, or where it had gone, were a continuous stream of stragglers of every description; women, children, and wounded and diseased soldiers, all hobbled pitifully after the troops. Through this mass struggled the overburdened, disorganized train, desperately trying to keep the ammunition

and supplies where they were needed. One hazard they faced were bands of deserters who were ready to take all they needed from these vulnerable supply trains, destroying what they could not carry.

The men in the ranks – the common soldiers – would have little idea of what they were fighting for – but then it really did not matter, for there was no room for personal initiative until the very last moment. Roles were clear, the infantryman didn't, as an individual, have any identity whatsoever, and with hundreds and hundreds of fellows about him, together only formed a very small piece in the bloody game of war. The moves were obscure and the purpose baffling, and all the soldier understood was his physical predicament which was clearly and uncomfortably dangerous.

Remember that in those times it was days not minutes that mattered. The artillery would carefully choose its targets amid the glittering ranks which confronted it, and their first target was often as not the infantry, standing rigidly to attention, totally exposed, and in unpleasantly dense formation. The havoc can be readily imagined, as up to 12 lbs of iron tore and rent its way through the massed lines, scattering bodies and limbs like tenpins in its wake. No one under any circumstances other than death or grievous wound was permitted to break rank, and the NCOs and officers beat back into line the less staunch but more practical men who felt that

14

anywhere in the opposite direction to that which they were about to go would be eminently more suitable.

We learn from memoires of his period that the only visible cannon balls as they came flying towards one's lines, was the one that was about to strike inches away; we can safely assume that those hit by roundshot also saw it coming. As it flew, only the shrieking sound of its passage through the air and then through muscle and bone identified it. All the while this pounding continued, the French guns would be answering with equal vigour and considerably more destruction. Their great grinding base roar and shrill piercing whistle filled the air, mingling with the agonized cries of the dying. The battle had begun.

With great curling rolls of smoke obscuring the battlefield, the order would finally come to advance. Drums beating the 'pas de charge', the infantry would close the gaps caused by casualties in the ranks as it moved forward. Overhead, the artillery barrage would continue until the last minute, shredding the enemy lines in preparation for the infantry assault. It was not unusual in the pandemonium for the artillery to mistime this vital arrangement and, smoke hiding the result, keep firing until their own regiments were suffering as many casualties as the foe.

The pace of the advance would quicken as the drum beats grew faster. Before the fusiliers, the voltigeurs would be spread thin and wide, running and firing as opportunity arose. Peppering the stiff enemy lines at increasingly close quarters, they could cause havoc; not only by the casualties they caused, but also to the morale of the troops they fired upon who, unlike when being fired at by cannon, could clearly see their assailants, but could not fire back, despite the proximity. Officers could only grit their teeth as they watched the nerves of their men slowly reach breaking point as they scowled at the darting figures that poured death at them for it was senseless wasting a volley on such dispersed targets weaving about the landscape. As the muskets took a fair while to load and the best ploy was to hold one's fire until the solid fusilier or grenadier ranks were almost upon one, fire, then follow through quickly with the bayonet. The voltigeurs' double role was to give French infantry regiments a tremendous advantage from their inception, but was not imitated until around 1809.

Back in the fusilier and grenadier columns all identity would be lost to the rhythm of the drums. Men fell screaming, clutching at fatal wounds, officers barked orders as shot and grapeshot filled the minute spaces between the men. The whole scene would be characterised by dense and often suffocating smoke and a sweltering heat that blinded the senses. With too many sensations for the mind to absorb, their feet propelled them forward, struck dumb with fear, white knuckles gripping tightly upon the one reality, the musket.

3: Line Infantry Regiments

BEFORE studying the uniforms of Napoleon's infantry in detail it is useful to have a compendium of each individual regiment of the Line. Owing to their large number this has necessarily been reduced to note form but should be a useful source of reference. Beneath each regimental number will be found its name of origin and the date upon which it was originally raised. Below this is its outline history in so far as the Napoleonic period is concerned. In italics are the battles in which each respective regiment takes part.

The 1st Line Infantry Regiment
(Picardie, 1569)
1796: 1er Demi-Brigade d'Infanterie de Ligne.
1803: 1er Régiment d'Infanterie de Ligne.
1814: 1er Régiment d'Infanterie, Régiment du Roi.
1805–1810: Armée d'Italie et de Naples *(Caldiero; Sacile; Wagram)*.
1810–1812: Stationed in Spain *(Miranda; Arapiles)*.
1813: Defended St. Sebastian then joined the 6th Corps of the Grande Armée *(Lützen; Bautzen; Dresden; Leipzig)*.
1814: Part of the Armée de Lyons *(Les Echelles; St. Julien)*.
       Rejoined the 6th Corps of the Grande Armée *(Brienne; Sézanne; Montmirail; Vauchamps; Laon, Paris)*.
1815: *(Quatre-Bras; Waterloo)*.

The 2nd Line Infantry Regiment
(Provence, 1776)
1796: 2eme Demi-Brigade d'Infanterie de Ligne.
1803: 2eme Régiment d'Infanterie de Ligne.
1814: 2eme Régiment d'Infanterie, Régiment de la Reine.
1804–1805: Naval duty *(Cape Finisterre; Trafalgar)*.
1806–1807: Joins the Armée d'Italie.
1807–1808: Joins the Grande Armée.
1809–1810: Joins the 4th Corps of the Armées d'Allemagne et du Rhin *(Essling; Aspern; Wagram)*.
1812–1814: Joins the 2nd Corps of the Grande Armée *(Polotsk; Berezina; Dresden; Leipzig; La Rothière)*.
1815: Joins the Armée du Nord *(Fleurus; Mont St Jean)*.

The 3rd Line Infantry Regiment
(Piémont, 1569)
1796: 3eme Demi-Brigade d'Infanterie de Ligne.
1803: 3eme Régiment d'Infanterie de Ligne.
1814: 3eme Régiment d'Infanterie, Régiment du Dauphin.
1805: With the Grande Armée *(Hollabruenn; Austerlitz)*.

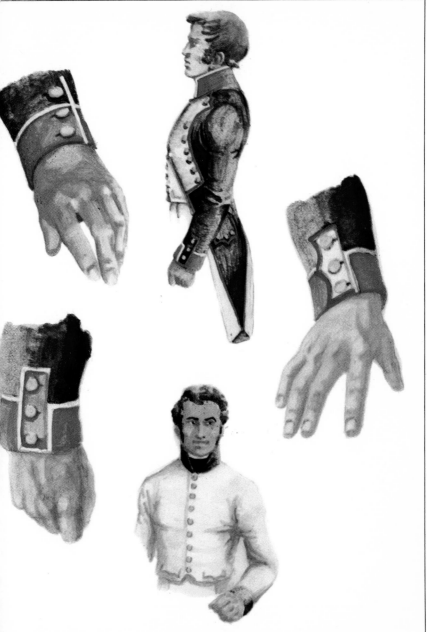

Detail of the habit-veste showing (upper left) the 1791 pattern cuff which was worn by some regiments up to 1812, (lower left) the more usual pattern flapped cuff and (lower right), an unusual scalloped flap more often used by Guard units. BOTTOM: Fatigue jacket or waistcoat worn under the habit-veste.

1807: Still with the Grande Armée *(Heilsberg; Friedland)*.
1809: Grande Armée *(Thorn; Schierling; Eckmuehl; Essling; Wagram)*.
1811–1813: Some battalions stationed in Spain.
1813: Four battalions clash with enemy at Goehrde.
1814: Campaign of France *(Bar-sur-Aube; Arcis-sur-Aube)*.
1815: *(Quatre-Bras; Waterloo)*.

The 4th Line Infantry Regiment
(Blaisois, 1776)
1796: 4eme Demi-Brigade d'Infanterie de Ligne.
1803: 4eme Régiment d'Infanterie de Ligne.
1814: 4eme Régiment d'Infanterie, Régiment de Monsieur.
1803–1805: Stationed at Boulogne.
1805: Joins 4th Corps of the Grande Armée *(Ulm; Austerlitz)*.
1806–1808: *(Jena; Eylau; Heilsberg; Koenigsberg)*.
1809: Joins the Armée d'Allemagne *(Eckmuehl; Aspern; Essling; Wagram)*.
1812: Joins 3rd Corps of the Grande Armée *(Smolensk; Valoutina; Moskowa; Krasnoe)*.
1813: 2nd Corps during the German campaign *(Dresden; Leipzig; Hanau)*.
1814: *(Brienne; La Rothière; Montereau; Troyes)*.
1815: Joins Armée du Nord's 2nd Corps *(Ligny)*.

The 5th Line Infantry Regiment
(Navarre, 1569)
1796: 5eme Demi-Brigade d'Infanterie de Ligne.
1803: 5eme Régiment d'Infanterie de Ligne.
1814: 5eme Régiment d'Infanterie, Régiment d'Angoulême.
1803–1805: Part of the Armeé d'Italie.
1806–1808: Stationed in Dalmatia.
1809–1810: *(Wagram)*.
           Croatian expedition.
1814: Stationed in Spain.
1815: *(Fleurus)*.

The 6th Line Infantry Regiment
(Armagnac, 1776)
1796: 6eme Demi-Brigade d'Infanterie de Ligne.
1803: 6eme Régiment d'Infanterie de Ligne.
1814: 6eme Régiment d'Infanterie, Régiment de Berry.
1803–1813: In the kingdom of Naples with the Armee d'Italie *(Calabres; Gayete; Reggio)*.
1813–1814: With the Grande Armée *(Mockern; Mersebourg; Wuerschen; Bautzen; Leipzig; Hanau)*.
           The 3rd battalion with the Armée d'Italie *(Mincio)*.
1815: Part of the Armée du Jura *(Belfort)*.

The 7th Line Infantry Regiment
(Champagne, 1559)
1796: 7eme Demi-Brigade d'Infanterie de Ligne.
1804: 7eme Régiment d'Infanterie de Ligne.
1814: 7eme Régiment d'Infanterie, Régiment d'Orléans.
1801–1804: Colonial service in San Domingo.
1808–1810: *(Passage of the Black Mountain, Barcelona, Salva, St Andre, Molins del Rey, Gerona, Villafranca)*.

The endless forced marches across the continent of Europe necessitated a garb far removed from that of the parade ground. The grenadiers in the fore-ground have wrapped their bearskins in waxed or oiled fabric and wear cumbersome greatcoats. Note the faggots tied to the pack of the right hand figure, a practical consideration for the speedy establishment of a bivouac. Note also that the officer behind them has replaced his bearskin with a more comfortable and convenient headgear, a bicorn. The bearskin hangs within the bag on his right hip (illustration from 'L'Epopee' by Job, courtesy of the National Army Museum).

Infantry in campaign dress. Note the bonnet de police (forage cap) and the fatigue dress of the left hand man. The centre man has a shako cover and wears brown trousers, characteristic of the Peninsular War. Note the different types of canteen in use.

Drum Majors in campaign dress, 1813.

1811: *(Tarragona; Fort Olivo)*.

1811–1813: *(Mont-Serrat, Sagonte, Valencia, Castella, Yecla, Falleja)*. With the Grande Armée, 7th Corps *(Bautzen; Jüterbock; Leipzig; Hanau; Tagliamento)*.

1815: *(Waterloo)*.

The 8th Line Infantry Regiment

(Austrasie, 1776)

1796: 8eme Demi-Brigade d'Infanterie de Ligne.

1814: 8eme Régiment d'Infanterie, Régment de Condé.

1802–1805: Part of the Armée de Hanovre.

1805–1808: Part of the 1st Corps of the Grande Armée *(Austerltz, Halle; Lubeck; Danzig, Friedland)*.

1808–1813: Part of the Armée d'Espagne *(Espinosa, Talavera-de-la Reina; Chiclana; Vittoria; Villalon)*.

1809: With the 2nd Corps of the Armées du rhin et d'Allemagne *(Essling; Wagram)*.

1814: Part of the 7th Corps of the Grande Armée *Bar-sur-Aubs; Arcis-Aube)*.

The 9th Line Infantry Regiment

(Normandie, 1615)

1796: 9eme Demi-Brigade d'Infanterie de Ligne.

1803: 9eme Régiment d'Infanterie de Ligne.

1814: 9eme Régiment d'Infanterie, Régiment de Bourbon.

1805: Part of the 5th Corps of the Grande Armée *(Hollabrünn; Austerlitz)*.

1806–1809: With the Armée d'Italie *(Venzione; Sacile; La Piave; Carlsdorf; Wagram)*.

1809–1810: Part of the Tyrol expedition.

1812–1813: Part of the 4th Corps of the Gramde Armée *(Vitebsk; Moskowa; Wiasma)*.

1813–1814: With the Armée d'Italie *(Mincio; Parma)*.

1815: Part of the Corps d'Observation du Var.

The 10th Line Infantry Regiment

(Neustrie, 1776)

1796: 10eme Demi-Brigade d'Infanterie de Ligne.

1803: 10eme Régiment d'Infanterie de Ligne.

1814: 10eme Régiment d'Infanterie, Régiment Colonel-General.

1803–1810: In Italy. 1805 campaign *(Castel-Franco)*.

1806: Part of the Armée de Naples *(Gayete)*.

1808: Conquest of Capri.

1810: Part of the corps of expedition in Sicily.

1811–1814: Navarre, Valencia and Aragon in Spain *(Siege of Valencia; Aranda de Sos; Deba)*.

1813–1814: 4th & 6th battalions with the Grande Armée *(Lützen; Bautzen; Goldberg; Leipzig; Hanau)*.

3rd, 5th & 7th battalions in Italy *(Caldiero; Mincio; Taro)*.

1815: With the Armée du Nord *(Waterloo)*.

The 11th Line Infantry Regiment

(La Marine, 1635)

1796: 11eme Demi-Brigade d'Infanterie de Ligne.

1803: 11eme Régiment d'Infanterie de Ligne.

A remarkably organized field hospital by Napoleonic standards. In actuality the 'operating table' would be surrounded with the crudest implements of surgery, saws and cleavers, and many amputated limbs. Little or no anaesthetic was available and most soldiers were more terrified of the attention of a surgeon than any number of enemy. Surgeons being so few and men in need of medical care so very many, the main consideration was speed. Gangrene infection was a known fatal result of delayed treatment. Thus amputation of any wounded limb was deemed the most effective remedy despite the brutal result of such treatment (from Job's 'L'Epopee', courtesy of the National Army Museum).

Musicien-Negre (Chapeau Chinois) of the 18th Regiment, 1805.

Two Tambour-Maitres and a Drum Major in the fantasy type uniforms adopted for the bands of some line infantry regiments before 1812. Note the fantasy details favoured by some colonels, in this instance light blue and crimson facings and two coloured braiding.

1805: *(Ulm; Gratz)*.
1806–1809: Part of the Armée de Dalmatie *(Sacille; Wagram; Znaim)*.
1811–1813: Spanish campaign *(Siege of Tortose)*.
1813: In Germany *(Siege of Wittenberg)*.
In Saxony *(Dresden; Leipzig; Hanau)*.
1814: Part of MacDonald's Corps during the French Campaign.
Restauration period spent in Savoie.
1815: *(Waterloo)*.

The 12th Line Infantry Regiment
(Auxerrois, 1692)
1796: 12eme Demi-Brigade d'Infanterie de Ligne.
1803: 12eme Régiment d'Infanterie de Ligne.
1805–1808: Gudin's division of the 3rd Corps of the Grande Armée *(Muehldorf; passageof La Salza: Austerlitz; Auerstaedt; Czarnowo; Pultusk; Eylau; Deppen; Friedland)*.
1809: Part of the Armée d'Allemagne *(Eckmuehl; Ratisbonne; Thann; Abensberg; Engerau; Wagram)*.
1810–1811: Spent in Magdebourg and Hannover.
1812: Gudin's then Gérard's division of the 1st Corps of the Grande Armée *(Vilna; Drissa; Vitebsk; Smolensk; Valoutina; Moskowa)*.
1813: In the 1st Division of the 1st Corps of the Grande Armée *(Hamburg; Dresden)*.
1814: The defence of Anvers *(Acris-sur-Aube; St Dizier)*.
1815: With the 5th Corps of the Armée du Nord *(Fleurus)*.

The 13th Line Infantry Regiment
(Bourbonnais, 1597)
1796: 13eme Demi-Brigade d'Infanterie de Ligne.
1803: 13eme Régiment d'Infanterie de Ligne.
1805: 8th Corps of the Armée d'Italie *(Caldiero)*.
1806: Part of the Corps d'Occupation du Istria.
1809: Part of MacDonald's Corps of the Armée d'Italie *(Isonzo Pass; Oberlaybach; Wagram)*.
1810: Helped quell the Tyrol uprising.
1813: Part of the 4th Corps of the Grande Armée *(Bautzen; Hanau; Hocheim)*.
1814: Defence of Mayence and Palma-Nova.
1815: Part of the Corps d'Observation des Pyrennes.

The 14th Line Infantry Regiment
(Forez, 1776)
1796: 14eme Demi-Brigade d'Infanterie de Ligne.
1803: 14eme Régiment d'Infanterie de Ligne.
1805: Part of the 4th Corps of the Grande Armée *(Ulm; Austerlitz)*.
1806–1807: Part of the 7th Corps of the Grande Armée *(Jena; Thorn; Eylau; Heilsberg)*.
1808–1814: 1st & 2nd battalions in Spain *(Saragossa; Villel; Tarragona; Valencia)*.
1813: 3rd & 4th battalions take part in the German campaign *(Lützen; Bautzen; Dresden; Wachau)*.
1814: The 5th battalion takes part in the French campaign *(Arcis-sur-Aube)*.

1815: The 1st & 2nd battalions form part of the Armée des Alpes
(Conflans; l'Hôpital).

The 15th Line Infantry Regiment
(Béarn, 1597)
1796: 15eme Demi-Brigade d'Infanterie de Ligne.
1803: 15eme Régiment d'Infanterie de Ligne.
1806: Joins the 8th Corps of the Grande Armée (Friedland).
1812: Stationed in Spain.

The 16th Line Infantry Regiment
(Agenois, 1776)
1801–1805: With the army of occupation in Brisgau.
1805: With the West Indies Fleet (Trafalgar).
1809: Part of the Armée d'Allemagne (Neumark; Ebersberg; Aspern;
Essling; Wagram; Znaïm).
1808–1812: With the Armée d'Espagne (Siege of Rosas; Siege of Gerona;
Capture of Fort Olivo; Siege of Tarragona; Mont-Serrat; Siege
of Sagonte; Siege of Valencia; San Felipe; Alicante).
1813–1814: Part of the Grande Armée (Lützen; Bautzen; Würschen;
Dresden; Leipzig).
1814: Part of the Armée de Lyons.

The 17th Line Infantry Regiment
(Auvergne, 1597)
1796: 17eme Demi-Brigade d'Infanterie de Ligne.
1803: 17eme Régiment d'Infanterie de Ligne.
1805: (Austerlitz).
1806–1808: With the Grande Armée and the Armée du Rhin (Eylau).
1809: At (Wagram) Colonel Oudet was mortally wounded.
1812: (Moskowa).
1813–1814: Defence of Dresden.
1815: (Waterloo).

The 18th Line Infantry Regiment
(Royal-Auvergne, 1776)
1796: 18eme Demi-Brigade d'Infanterie de Ligne.
1803: 18eme Régiment d'Infanterie de Ligne.
1805: Part of the 4th Corps of the Grande Armée (Hollabruenn; Austerlitz).
1806–1807: Still with the 4th Corps (Jena; Eylau; Heilsberg).
1809: 4th Corps (Ebersberg; Vienna; Essling; Wagram; Znaïm).
1812: Part of the 3rd Corps of the Grande Armée (Smolensk; Moskowa).
1813: Part of the 2nd Corps of the Grande Armée (Dresden; Leipzig;
Hanau).
1814: With the 2nd Corps during the French campaign (Magdebourg; La
Rothière; Montereau).
1815: Partof the Armée d'Alsace (Suerbourg; Strasbourg).

The 19th Line Infantry Regiment
(Flandres, 1597)
1796: 19eme Demi-Brigade d'Infanterie de Ligne.
1803: 19eme Régiment d'Infanterie de Ligne.
1804–1806: Part of the Armée de Hanovre.
1807–1809: With the 10th Corps of the Grande Armée (Siege of Danzig).

eur hornist in the green Imperial Livery which was decreed by the Bardin Regulations of 1812. Note the red shako decoration and red fringed epaulettes of the grenadier and the yellow and green ornaments of the voltigeur. Detail of the Imperial Livery lace — two variations — is shown inset.

28

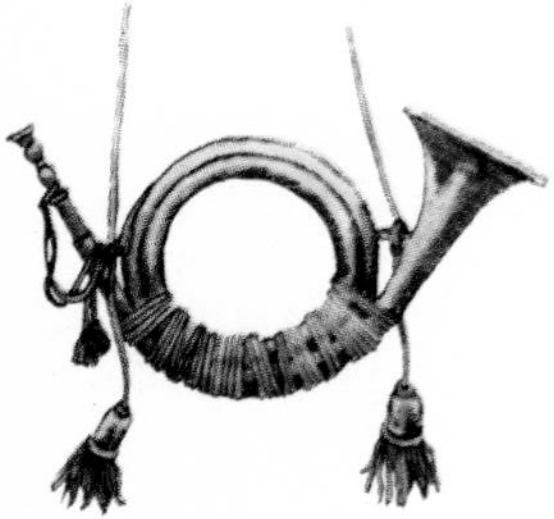

VALEUR
ET DISCIPLINE
4eme BATAILLON
L'EMPEREUR
DES FRANÇAIS,
AU 3eme RÉGIMENT
D'INFANTERIE
DE LIGNE

ABOVE: The eagle and standard of the 3rd Regiment of the Line, 1809. Both sides are shown. LEFT: A voltigeur bugle-horn and a regulation brass drum with pale blue rims.

Men of the 34th Regiment awake to the beat of a drum in a typically muddy field bivouac. Note the furled standard stacked with the muskets in the background on the left (illustration from Job's 'L'Epopee', courtesy of the National Army Museum).

1809: Joins the 9th Corps of the Armée d'Alemagne *(Wagram)*.
1810–1811: With the Armée d'Espagne et de Portugal *(Astorga; Busaco; Torres-Vedras)*.
1812: 2nd Corps of the Grande Armée *(Jacobouwo; Polotsk; Borisow)*.
1813: 2nd Corps of the Armee d'Allemagne *(Dresden; Leipzig)*.
1814: 2nd Corps during the French campaign *(Brienne; Montereau; Bar-sur-Aube)*.
1815: 1st Corps of the Armée du Nord *(Waterloo)*.

The 20th Line Infantry Regiment
(Cambrésis, 1776)
1796: 20eme Demi-Brigade d'Infanterie de Ligne.
1803: 20eme Régiment d'Infanterie de Ligne.
1805: Part of the Armée d'Italie *(Adige Pass; Caldiero)*.
1805–1810: Conquest of the Kingdom of Naples.
1811–1812: Part of the Armée d'Espagne *(Tarragona; Ciudad-Real; Valencia)*.
1813: 3 battalions joined the Armée d'Aragon.
    1 battalion joined the Armée d'Italie.
1814: 2 battalions joined the Armée de Lyons.

The 21st Line Infantry Regiment
(Guyenne, 1589)
1796: 21eme Demi-Brigade d'Infanterie de Ligne.
1803: 21eme Régiment d'Infanterie de Ligne.
1806–1808: Part of the 3rd Corps of the Grande Armée *(Auerstaedt; Pultusk; Eylau)*.
1809–1811: Part of the Armée d'Allemagne and the Rhine *(Eckmuehl; Wagram)*.
1812: With the 1st Corps of the Grande Armée *(Smolensk; Valoutina; Moskowa)*.
1813: *(Dresden)*.
1814: *(Berg-op-Zoom)*.
1815: Part of the 1st Corps of the Armee du Nord *(Waterloo)*.

The 22nd Line Infantry Regiment
(Viennois, 1776)
1796: 22eme Demi-Brigade d'Infanterie de Ligne.
1803: 22eme Régiment d'Infanterie de Ligne.
1806–1807: With the 8th Corps of the Grande Armée *(Stralsund; Heilsberg)*.
1809–1813: With the Armées de Portugal and d'Espagne. *(Astorga; St Sebastien)*.
1813: With the 3rd Corps of the Grande Armée *(Luetzen, Bautzen)*.
1815: Fought in the French campaign *(Fleurus and Wavre)*.

The 23rd Line Infantry Regiment
(Royal, 1656).
1796: 23eme Demi-Brigade d'Infanterie de Ligne.
1803: 23eme Régiment d'Infanterie de Ligne.
1805: With the Armée d'Italie *(Caldiero)*.
1807–1809: Part of the Illyrian and Dalmation expeditions *(Raguse; Albania)*.
1809: Part of the Armée d'Allemagne *(Wagram)*.

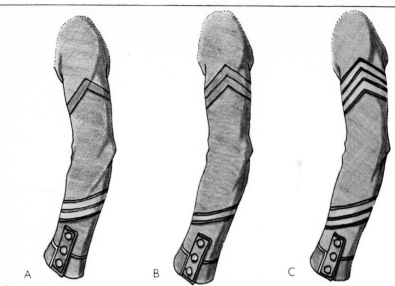

Rank insignia and long service chevrons: (A) Corporal – two golden yellow wool bars above each cuff on red cloth, one red chevron indicating a single period of service. (B) Sergeant – one gold braid bar on red cloth above each cuff on red cloth. Two red chevrons indicating a double period of engagement. (C) Sergeant-Major – two gold braid bars on red cloth above each cuff on red cloth, the gold chevrons indicating a treble period of service.

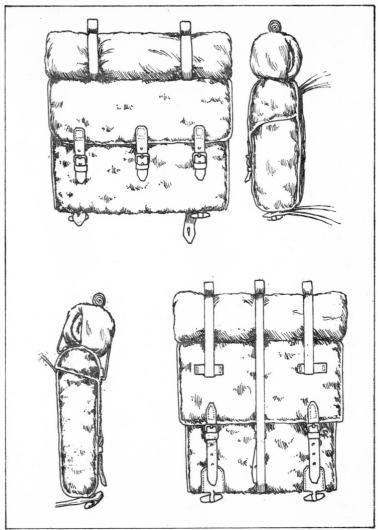

ABOVE: Two different styles of knapsack showing the toggles to which the straps were attached and the rolled greatcoat on the top of the pack.

1812: With the Armée d'Espagne.
1813: With the Grande Armée at *(Luetzen)* and *(Bautzen)*.
1815: Part of the Armée du Nord *(Ligny; Wavre)*.

The 24th Line Infantry Regiment
(Brie, 1775)
1796: 24eme Demi-Brigade d'Infanterie de Ligne.
1803: 24eme Régiment d'Infanterie de Ligne.
1805: In Tyrol during the Austrian campaign.
1806: Prussian campaign *(Jena)*.

1807: Polish campaign *(Pultusk; Golymin; Eylau; Braunsberg; Friedland)*.
1808–1812: The 1st, 2nd and 3rd battalions were in Spain *(Espinosa; Somo-Sierra; Madrid; Uclés; Medellin; Talavera; Cadix)*.
1809: The 4th battalion took part in the Austrian campaign *(Essling; Wagram)*.
1813: The 1st battalion remained in Spain *(Vuinca; the Pyrennes campaign)*.
    The 2nd battalion was part of the Corps d'Observation in Bavaria.
    The 3rd battalion took part in the German campaign *(Dresden)*.
    The 4th battalion was part of the Corps d'Occupation at Danzig.
1814: The 1st battalion took part in the French campaign *(Mormant; Méry; Craonne; Laon; Reims; St Dizier)*.
    The 2nd and 6th battalions fought in France also *(defence of Lyons; St Julien; St Georges; Limonest)*.
    The 3rd battalion fought at *(Dresden)*.
    The 4th at *(Danzig)*.
    The 5th defended *(Besançon)*.
1815: The 1st, 2nd, 5th and 6th battalions defended Savoie *(Montmélian)*.

The 25th Line Infantry Regiment
(Poitou, 1616)
1796: 25eme Demi-Brigade d'Infanterie de Ligne.
1803: 25eme Régiment d'Infanterie de Ligne.
1805–1808: With the 3rd Corps of the Grande Armée *(Steyer; Austerlitz; Auerstaedt; Pultusk; Eylau; Koenigsberg)*.
1809–1810: Part of the Armée d'Allemagne and that of the Rhine *(Landshut; Eckmuehl; Ratisbonne; Wagram)*.
1812–1813: Part of the 1st Corps of the Grande Armée*(Minsk; Smolensk; Moskowa; Hamburg; Dresden)*.
1814: Formed part of the defence force of Paris.
1815: With the 1st Corps of the Armée du Nord *(Waterloo)*.

The 26th Line Infantry Regiment
(Bresse, 1775)
1796: 26eme Demi-Brigade d'Infanterie de Ligne.
1803: 26eme Régiment d'Infanterie de Ligne.
1805: The 1st and 2nd battalions formed part of the expedition to Dominique.
1805–1814: These same stationed in Guadeloupe and Martinique.
1807–1813: The other battalions part of the Armée de Portugal *(Algarves; Beja; Evora; Rorissa; Vimiero; Francellos; Orense; Avedes; Lambroso; Oporte; Ponte-de-Lima; Ciudad-Rodrigo; Almeida; Busaco; Punhete; Castel-Branco; Redinha)*.
1813: *(Vittoria)*.
1813–1814: Part of the Armée des Pyrennes *(Altobiscar; Cubiry; Berra; La Baïonette)*.
1813–1814: With the Grande Armée *(Luetzen; Bautzen; Jauer; Dresden; Leipzig)*.
1814–1815: Part of the Armée de la Vendée.

The 27th Line Infantry Regiment
(Lyonnais, 1616)

1796: 27eme Demi-Brigade d'Infanterie de Ligne.

1803: 27eme Régiment d'Infanterie de Ligne.

1805–1807: With the Grande Armée *(Guensburg; Ulm; the Tyrolean expedition; Scharnitz; Zell; Eylau; Friedland; Danzig).*

1808: With the Armée d'Espagne *(Bubierca).*

1809: With the Armée d'Allemagne *(Essling; Wagram).*

1811–1812: With the Armée de Portugal *(Redinha; Almeida; Arapiles).*

1813: Part of the 14th Corps of the Grande Armée *(Luetzen; Dresden).*

1815: With the Armée du Nord at *(Waterloo).*

The 28th Line Infantry Regiment

(Maine, 1775)

1796: 28eme Demi-Brigade d'Infanterie de Ligne.

1803: 28eme Régiment d'Infanterie de Ligne.

1805: With the 4th Corps of the Grande Armée *(Austerlitz).*

1806–1807: With the Grande Armée *(Lübeck; Bergfried; Eylau; Heilsberg).*

1808–1813: With the Armées de Portugal and d'Espagne *(Talavera; Almonacid).*

1814: Part of the Grande Armée during the French campaign.

1815: Part of the Armée du Nord at *(Waterloo).*

The 29th Line Infantry Regiment

(Dauphin, 1667)

1796: 29eme Demi-Brigade d'Infanterie de Ligne.

1803: 29eme Régiment d'Infanterie de Ligne.

Part of Lamarque's Division at *(Wagram)* where the 29th lost 70 officers and three-quarters of the men.

1812: Fought at *(Wilna)* during the Russian campaign.

1813: *(Danzig).*

1815: Part of the Armée du Nord *(Waterloo).*

The 30th Line Infantry Regiment

(Perche, 1775)

1796: 30eme Demi-Brigade d'Infanterie de Ligne.

1803: 30eme Régiment d'Infanterie de Ligne.

1805–1808: Part of the 3rd Corps of the Grande Armée *(Ulm; Lambach; Austerlitz; Auerstaedt; Heilsberg; Eylau).*

1809–1810: With the Armées d'Allemagne and that of the Rhine *(Landshut; Eckmuehl; Essling; Wagram).*

1812: Took part in the Russian campaign *(Smolensk; Wiasma; Krasnoe).* At the battle of *(Borodino)* the 30th lost 44 officers and two-thirds of the men storming the great redoubt.

1813–1814: With the 13th Corps of the Grande Armée. Stationed in Hamburg.

1815: Part of the Armée du Nord *(Ligny).*

The 31st Line Infantry Regiment

(Aunis, 1610)

1796: 31eme Demi-Brigade d'Infanterie de Ligne.

1801–1804: Part of the San Domingo expedition.

1804: The Regiment was absorbed into the 7th and 105th Line Infantry Regiments.

The 32nd Line Infantry Regiment
(Bassigny, 1775)
1796: 32eme Demi-Brigade d'Infanterie de Ligne.
1803: 32eme Régiment d'Infanterie de Ligne.
1805–1807: With the Grande Armée *(Haslach; Diernstein; Ulm; Halle; Braunsberg; Friedland).*
1808–1814: With the Armée d'Espagne.
1815: With the Armée du Rhin *(Mundolsheim).*

The 33rd Line Infantry Regiment
(Touraine, 1625)
1796: 33eme Demi-Brigade d'Infanterie de Ligne.
1803: 33eme Régiment d'Infanterie de Ligne.
1803: With the Armée des Côtes.
1805–1808: Part of the 3rd Corps of the Grande Armée *(Austerlitz; Auerstaedt; Eylau; Danzig).*
1809–1810: Pat of the Armées d'Allemagne et du Rhin *(Eckmuehl; Wagram; Stettin).*
1812–1813: Part of the 1st Corps of the Grande Armée *(Moskowa; Kulm).*
1814: Stationed in Luxemburg.
1815: Part of the 3rd Corps of the Armée du Nord *(Ligny).*

The 34th Line Infantry Regiment
(Angoulême, 1775)
1796: 34eme Demi-Brigade d'Infanterie de Ligne.
1803: 34eme Régiment d'Infanterie de Ligne.
1805–1807: With the Grande Armée *(Ulm; Austerlitz; Saalfeld; Jena; Pultusk; Ostrolenka; Friedland).*
1809–1812: With the Armée d'Espagne *(Saragossa; Lucena; Jaca; Arzobispo; Ocana; Badajoz; Gebora; Arroyo-del-Molinos; Burgos).*
1813–1814: With the Armée des Pyrennés *(San Sebastian; Bayonne; Orthez; Toulouse).*
1815: With the Armée du Nord *(Fleurus).*

The 35th Line Infantry Regiment
(Aquitaine, 1625)
1799: 35eme Demi-Brigade d'Infanterie de Ligne.
1803: 35eme Régiment d'Infanterie de Ligne.
1803–1804: At the camp of Utrecht.
1805: With the 2nd Corps of the Grande Armée *(Ulm; Vienna).*
1809: With the Armée d'Italie *(Raab; Wagram; Pardenone).*
1812: In Russia *(Smolensk; Moskowa).*
1813–1814: With the Armée d'Italie *(Mincio; Parma).*

The 36th Line Infantry Regiment
(Anjou, 1775)
1796: 36eme Demi-Brigade d'Infanterie de Ligne.
1803: 36eme Régiment d'Infanterie de Ligne.
1805–1808: Part of the 4th Corps of the Grande Armée *(Ulm; Austerlitz; Jena; Eylau; Heilsberg).*
1808–1809: In Spain *(Burgos; Corunna).*

1810–1813: Part of the Armée de Portugal *(Xeres; Busaco; Arapiles, Vittoria)*.
1814: Part of the Armées d'Espagne et des Pyrennés *(Toulouse)*.
1815: With the Armée du Rhin.

The 37th Line Infantry Regiment
(Maréchal-de-Turenne, 1625)
1796: 37eme Demi-Brigade d'Infanterie de Ligne.
1803: 37eme Régiment d'Infanterie de Ligne.
1807–1808: In Spain *(Gerona)*.
1809: In Germany *(Essling; Wagram)*.
1811: In Spain *(Tarragona)*.
1812: In Russia *(Moskowa; Polotsk)*.
1813: In Germany *(Luetzen; Bautzen; Hamburg)*.
1814: Part of the 2nd Corps of the Grande Armée *(La Rothière, Montereau)*.
1815: *(Fleurus; Waterloo)*.

The 38th Line Infantry Regiment
(Dauphiné, 1629)
Vacant during the Empire.

The 39th Line Infantry Regiment
(Isle-de-France, 1629)
1796: 39eme Demi-Brigade d'Infanterie de Ligne.
1803: 39eme Régiment d'Infanterie de Ligne.
1805–1807: With the Grande Armée *(Elchingen; Jena; Eylau; Friedland)*.
1808–1814: In Spain *(Busaco; Torres-Vedras; Fuentes d'Onoro; Arapiles)*.
In Germany *(Essling; Dresden)*.
The 4th battalion only *(Wagram; Danzig)*.
1814: *(Toulouse)*.

The 40th Line Infantry Regiment
(Soisonnais, 1630)
1796: 40eme Demi-Brigade d'Infanterie de Ligne.
1803: 40eme Régiment d'Infanterie de Ligne.
1805–1808: Part of the Grande Armée *(Michelsberg; Hollabruenn; Austerlitz; Saalfeld; Jena; Ostrolenka)*.
1808–1814: In Spain *(Saragossa, Arzobispo; Ocana; Albufera; Toulouse)*.
The 4th battalion *(Ebersberg; Essling; Wagram)*.
The 3rd battalion *(Luetzen; Bautzen; Leipzig; Champaubert; Vauchamps; Paris)*.

The 41st Line Infantry Regiment
(La Reine, 1634)
1796: 41eme Demi-Brigade d'Infanterie de Ligne.
1803: Amalgamated into the 17th Line Infantry Regiment.

The 42nd Line Infantry Regiment
(Limousin, 1635)
1796: 42eme Demi-Brigade d'Infanterie de Ligne.

1803: 42eme Régiment d'Infanterie de Ligne.
1803–1805: Part of the Corps d'Occupation in Taranto.
1806: With the Armée de Naples *(Reggio)*.
1807: Part of the Armée d'Italie *(Bologna; Verona)*.
1808–1811: With the Armée d'Espagne *(Villa-Rodonia; Gerona; Vich; Tarragona)*.
1809: Some battalions with the Armée d'Italie *(Raab; Wagram)*.
1813: Part of the Grande Armée *(Bautzen; Lukau; Grossbeeren; Dennewitz)*.
1813–1814: Back with the Armée d'Italie.

The 43rd Line Infantry Regiment
(Royal-Vaisseaux, 1638)
1796: 43eme Demi-Brigade d'Infanterie de Ligne.
1803: 43eme Régiment d'Infanterie de Ligne.
1806–1808: Part of the 4th Corps of the Grande Armée *(Jena)*.
1808–1814: With the Armée d'Espagne *(Bilbao; Osuna)*.
1814: Part of Marmont's 6th Corps *(Champaubert; Montmirail; Vauchamps; Laon)*.

The 44th Line Infantry Regiment
(Orléans, 1642)
1796: 44eme Demi-Brigade d'Infanterie de Ligne.
1803: 44eme Régiment d'Infanterie de Ligne.
1805: Part of the Armée des Côtes, Brest.
1806–1808: Part of the 7th Corps of the Grande Armée *(Jena; Pultusk; Eylau; Danzig)*.
1808–1812: Part of the Armée d'Espagne *(Sarragossa; Tudela; Tortosa; Sagonte; Valencia)*.
1815: With the Armée du Nord *(Fleurus)*.

The 45th Line Infantry Regiment
(Régiment de la Couronne, 1643)
1796: 45eme Demi-Brigade d'Infanterie de Ligne.
1803: 45eme Régiment d'Infanterie de Ligne.
1803–1804: Part of the Armée de Hanovre.
1805–1807: Part of the 1st Corps of the Grande Armée *(Austerlitz; Halle; Lubeck; Mohrungen; Friedland)*.
1808–1813: With the Armées d'Espagne et de Portugal *(Talavera; Almonacid)*.
1813–1814: Some battalions with the Armée d'Espagne at *(Toulouse)*.
The rest with the 14th Corps of the Grande Armée *(Dresden)*.
1815: With the Armée du Nord *(Waterloo)*.

The 46th Line Infantry Regiment
(Bretagne, 1644)
1796: 46eme Demi-Brigade d'Infanterie de Ligne.
1803: 46eme Régiment d'Infanterie de Ligne.
1805–1807: Part of the 4th Corps of the Grande Armée *(Ulm; Austerlitz; Jena; Lubeck; Eylau; Heilsberg)*.
1809: Still with the 4th Corps *(Essling; Wagram; Znaïm)*.

1812-1814: With the 3rd Corps of the Grande Armée *(Smolensk; Valoutina; Moskowa; Wiasma; Krasnoe).*
With the 1st & 2nd Corps at *(Kulm; Leipzig; Hanau).*
With the 2nd Corps at *(Brienne; La Rothière; Montereau; Bar-sur-Aube).*
1815: Part of the 1st Corps of the Armée du Nord *(Waterloo).*

The 47th Line Infantry Regiment

(Lorraine, 1644)
1798: 47eme Demi-Brigade d'Infanterie de Ligne.
1803: 47eme Régiment d'Infanterie de Ligne.
1803–1808: Naval duty on board the *Regulus* and the *President.*
1808–1814: In Spain *(Evora; Vimiero; Pampelune; Saragossa; Medina-del-Rio-Seco; Corunna; Porto; Astorga; Almeida; Torres-Vedras; Salamanca; Vittoria; Pampelune; Orthez; Toulouse).*
1813: The 3rd, 4th and 5th battalions were part of the Armée d'Allemagne *(Luetzen; Bautzen; Leipzig).*

The 48th Line Infantry Regiment

(Artois, 1610)
1796: 48eme Demi-Brigade d'Infanterie de Ligne.
1803: 48eme Régiment d'Infanterie de Ligne.
1805–1809: Part of the 3rd Corps of the Grande Armée *(Austerlitz; Auerstaedt; Nasielsk; Eylau; Eckmuehl; Wagram).*
1812: With the 1st Corps of the Grande Armée *(Moskowa; Krasnoe; Berezina).*
1813: With the 13th Corps of the Armée de l'Elbe *(Hamburg).*
1815: Part of the 4th Corps of the Armée du Nord *(Ligny).*

The 49th Line Infantry Regiment

(Vintimille, 1647)
1796: 49eme Demi-Brigade d'Infanterie de Ligne.
1803: Dissolved until the Restoration in 1814.

The 50th Line Infantry Regiment

(Hainaut, 1651)
1796: 50eme Demi-Brigade d'Infanterie de Ligne.
1803: 50eme Régiment d'Infanterie de Ligne.
1805–1808: Part of the 6th Corps of the Grande Armée *(Ulm; Scharnitz; Erfurt; Jena; Magdebourg; Eylau; Friedland).*
1808–1812: With the Armées d'Espagne et de Portugal *(Banios, Ciudad-Rodrigo; Redinha).*
1813: Part of the 3rd Corps of the Grande Armée *(Lützen; Bautzen; Dresden; Hanau).*
1814: In France *(Toulouse; Champaubert; Montmirail; Vauchamps).*
1815: *(Ligny).*

The 51st Line Infantry Regiment

(La Sarre, 1651)
1796: 51eme Demi-Brigade d'Infanterie de Ligne.
1803: 51eme Régiment d'Infanterie de Ligne.

1805–1807: With the Grande Armée *(Austerlitz; Auerstaedt; Czarnovo; Golymin; Eylau; Ostrolenka; Danzig; Friedland)*.

1808–1813: In Spain *(Madrid; Valencia; Bilbao; Talavera; Almonacid; Fuente-Ovejuna; Albufera; Tarifa; Cadix; Vittoria; Maya)*.

1812–1813: Some battalions with the Grande Armée at *(Borizow; Kulm; Dresden)*.

1813–1814: In Holland *(Arnheim; Berg-op-Zoom; Courtray)*.

1814: Part of the Armée des Pyrennés *(Orthez; Toulouse)*.

1815: With the Armée du Nord at *(Waterloo)*.

The 52nd Line Infantry Regiment

(La Fère, 1654)

1796: 52eme Demi-Brigade d'Infanterie de Ligne.

1803: 52eme Régiment d'Infanterie de Ligne.

1805: Part of the Armée d'Italie *(Verona; Caldiero)*.

1806–1808: Stationed in Italy and Hungary *(Wagram)*.

1811–1813: In Germany *(Bautzen; Hanau)*.

1814: In Italy *(Genoa)*.

1815: Part of the Corps d'Occupation du Jura.

The 53rd Line Infantry Regiment

(Alsace, 1656)

1796: 53eme Demi-Brigade d'Infanterie de Ligne.

1803: 53eme Régiment d'Infanterie de Ligne.

1805–1806: With the Armée d'Italie *(Caldiero; Tagliamento; Tyrolean expedition)*.

1808–1809: Still with the Armée d'Italie *(Piave passage; Tagliamento passage; San-Michele; Raab; Wagram; Znaïm)*.

1812: In Russia *(Witepsk; Moskowa; Malojaroslawetz; Krasnoe)*.

1813–1814: Back with the Armée d'Italie *(Caldiero; San-Michele; Boara; Mincio)*.

The 54th Line Infantry Regiment

(Royal-Roussillon, 1657)

1796: 54eme Demi-Brigade d'Infanterie de Ligne.

1803: 54eme Régiment d'Infanterie de Ligne.

1805: With the 1st Corps of the Grande Armée *(Austerlitz)*.

1806–1807: Still with the 1st Corps *(Friedland)*.

1808–1812: Part of the Armée d'Espagne *(Espinosa; Somo-Sierra; Talavera; Chiclana)*.

1813: 2 battalions served in Germany, 1 battalion served in Spain.

1814: The 1st battalion served in the French campaign *(Fère-Champenoise)*.

1815: Part of the Armée du Nord *(Waterloo)*.

The 55th Line Infantry Regiment

(Condé, 1644)

1796: 55eme Demi-Brigade d'Infanterie de Ligne.

1803: 55eme Régiment d'Infanterie de Ligne.

1805–1807: With the Grande Armée *(Austerlitz; Jena; Eylau; Heilsberg)*.

1808–1812: In Spain *(Albufera)*.

1812: In Russia with the Grande Armée *(Berezina)*.

1813: With the Grande Armée *(Bautzen; Dresden; Kulm)*.

1812–1814: Some battalions with the Armée d'Espagne *(Vittoria; Orthez; Toulouse)*.
1815: Part of the Armée du Nord *(Fleurus; Waterloo)*.

The 56th Line Infantry Regiment
(Bourbon, 1635)
1796: 56eme Demi-Brigade d'Infanterie de Ligne.
1803: 56eme Régiment d'Infanterie de Ligne.
1805: Part of the Armée d'Italie *(Caldiero)*.
1807: With the Grande Armée *(Stettin; Stralsund)*.
1808–1809: In Spain *(Rosas; Gerona)*.
1809: With the Grande Armée *(Eckmuehl; Essling; Wagram)*.
1812: Still with the Grande Armée *(Dunaburg; Polotsk; Berezina)*.
1813: In Saxony *(Dresden; Leipzig; Hanau)*.
1814: In France *(Brienne; La Rothière; Montereau)*.
1815: Part of the Armée du Nord *(Ligny; Wavre)*.

The 57th Line Infantry Regiment
(Beauvoisis, 1667)
1796: 57eme Demi-Brigade d'Infanterie de Ligne.
1803: 57eme Régiment d'Infanterie de Ligne.
1805–1806: With the Grande Armée *(Memmingen; Ulm; Austerlitz; Jena; Lubeck)*.
1807: Still with the Grande Armée *(Bergfried; Deppen; Hoff; Eylau; Lomitten; Heilsberg)*.
1809: Still part of the Grande Armée *(Thann; Abensberg; Eckmuehl; Ratisbonne; Essling; Wagram)*.
1812: In Russia *(Mohilow; Moskowa; Malojaroslavetz; Viasma; Krasnoe)*.
1805–1806: With the Grande Armée *Memmingen; Ulm; Austerlitz; Jena;*
1814: Defence of Strasbourg.

The 58th Line Infantry Regiment
(Rouergue, 1667)
1796: 58eme Demi-Brigade d'Infanterie de Ligne.
1803: 58eme Régiment d'Infanterie de Ligne.
1806–1807: With the Grande Armée *(Heilsberg; Friedland)*.
1808–1814: In Spain *(Vimiero; Valmeida; Talavera; Almonacid; Ocana; Albufera; Vittoria; Toulouse)*.
1813: Some battalions in Germany *(Luetzen; Wurschen; Dresden)*.
1814: In France *(Montereau; Paris)*.

The 59th Line Infantry Regiment
(Bourgogne, 1668)
1798: 59eme Demi-Brigade d'Infanterie de Ligne.
1803: 59eme Régiment d'Infanterie de Ligne.
1805–1808: With the Grande Armée *(Guntzburg; Ulm; Austerlitz; Jena; Friedland)*.
1808–1814: Some battalions with the Armées d'Espagne et du Portugal *(Tudela; Col de Banios; Ciudad-Rodrigo; Fuentes d'Onoro; Arapiles; Vittoria; Orthez; Toulouse)*.
1809: Some battalions in Germany *(Ebensberg; Essling; Wagram)*.
1813–1814: With the Armée d'Allemagne *(Luetzen; Bautzen; Dresden; Leipzig; Danzig)*.
1815: Part of the Armée du Nord *(Fleurus; Ligny)*.

The 60th Line Infantry Regiment
(Royal-Marine, 1669)
1796: 60eme Demi-Brigade d'Infanterie de Ligne.
1803: 60eme Régiment d'Infanterie de Ligne.
1805: In Italy *(Caldiero)*.
1806–1809: In Dalmatia, Albania & Illyria *(Raab; Wagram; Znaïm)*.
1812: In Spain *(Valencia; Tordesillas)*.
1812–1813: Part of the Armée de Catalogne *(Col Sacro; Roda; La Salud)*.

The 61st Line Infantry Regiment
(Vermandois, 1669)
1796: 61eme Demi-Brigade d'Infanterie de Ligne.
1803: 61eme Régiment d'Infanterie de Ligne.
1803–1812: Part of the Grande Armée at the following battles:
1805: *(Dachau; Muhldorf; Lambach; Austerlitz)*.
1806: *(Auerstaedt)*.
1807: In Poland *(Eylau; Ostrolenka; Guttstadt)*.
1809: In Austria *(Ratisbonne; Abensberg; Landshut; Essling; Wagram)*.
1812: In Russia *(Mohilow; Viasma; Schwardino; Moskowa)*.
1813: Part of the Armée de l'Elbe *(Defence of Hamburg)*.
1815: *(Quatre-Bras; Waterloo)*.

The 62nd Line Infantry Regiment
(Salm-Salm, 1667)
1796: 62eme Demi-Brigade d'Infanterie de Ligne.
1803: 62eme Régiment d'Infanterie de Ligne.
1805–1809: In Italy *(Caldiero; Siege of Gaëte)*.
1809: In Austria *(Raab; Wagram)*.
1811–1813: In Spain *(Les Arapiles; Logroño; San Sebastien)*.
1813: In Germany *(Lützen; Bautzen)*.

The 63rd Line Infantry Regiment
(Ernest, 1672)
1797: 63eme Demi-Brigade d'Infanterie de Ligne.
1803: 63eme Régiment d'Infanterie de Ligne.
1805–1807: With the Grande Armée *(Eylau; Friedland)*.
1808–1814: In Spain *(Chiclana)*.
1813: Some battalions in Germany *(Leipzig)*.
1815: *(Fleurus)*.

The 64th Line Infantry Regiment
(Salis-Samande, 1672)
1796: 64eme Demi-Brigade d'Infanterie de Ligne.
1803: 64eme Régiment d'Infanterie de Ligne.
1805: Part of the Grande Armée *(Michelsberg; Ulm; Austerlitz)*.
1806–1807: *(Saalfeld; Jena; Pultusk; Ostrolenka)*.
1808–1814: In Spain *(Saragossa; Ocana; Olivencia; Badajoz; Albufera)*.
            The 1st & 2nd battlions at *(Bayonne)*.
1813: The 3rd & 4th battalions with the Grande Armée *(Dresden)*.
1815: Part of the 3rd Corps of the Armée du Nord *(Ligny; Namur; Dinant)*.

The 65th Line Infantry Regiment
(Sonnenberg, 1672)
1799: 65eme Demi-Brigade d'Infanterie de Ligne.

1803: 65eme Régiment d'Infanterie de Ligne.
1806: Part of the Armée du Nord.
1806–1808: With the 8th Corps of the Grande Armée *(Stralsund; Allenstein; Heilsberg)*.
1808–1809: Part of the Armée du Rhin *(Ratisbonne; Essling; Wagram; Flessingue)*.
1810–1813: With the Armées de Portugal et d'Espagne *(Astorga; Sobral; Rio-Major; Fuentes d'Onoro; Salamanca; Castro; Vittoria)*.
1813: Part of the Grande Armée *(Lützen; Bautzen; Dresden; Leipzig)*.
1814: In France *(Bayonne; Orthez; Toulouse)*.
1815: Operations in the Vendée *(Namur)*.

The 66th Line Infantry Regiment
(Castella, 1672)
1796: 66eme Demi-Brigade d'Infanterie de Ligne.
1803: 66eme Régiment d'Infanterie de Ligne.
1805–1806: Part of the Armée des Côtes de l'Ocean.
1807: With the first expedition to Portugal.
1808: Part of the expedition to Guadeloupe.
1808–1813: Part of the 2nd Corps of the Armée de Portugal *(Oporto)*.
With the 6th Corps of the Armée de Portugal *(Ciudad-Rodrigo; Busaco; Torres Vedras; Fuentes d'Onoro; Salamanca; Arapiles; Tolosa)*.
1813–1814: With the Armée d'Espagne.
1813: The 5th battalion with the Grande Armée *(Lützen; Bautzen; Leipzig; Hanau)*.
1814: Part of the 6th Corps of the Armée du Nord *(Fère Champenoise; defence of Paris)*.
1815: With the Corps d'Observation des Pyrennés, excepting for three battalions on service in Guadeloupe.

The 67th Line Infantry Regiment
(Languedoc, 1672)
1796: 67eme Demi-Brigade d'Infanterie de Ligne.
1803: 67eme Régiment d'Infanterie de Ligne.
1804–1805: Naval service *(Trafalgar)*.
1807: Part of the Armée de Reserve in Pomerania *(Stralsund)*.
1807–1810: Part of the Grande Armée *(Essling; Wagram)*.
1808–1814: With the Armée de Catalogne *(Gerona; Villafranca; St Privat)*.
1813: Part of the Grande Armée at *(Lützen; Bautzen)*.
1814: Part of the Armée d'Italie at *(Mincio; Gênes)*.
1814: Part of the Armée de Lyon *(Mâcon; Lyon)*.
1815: With the Armée des Alpes.

The 68th Line Infantry Regiment
(Beauce, 1673)
1796: 68eme Demi-Brigade d'Infanterie de Ligne.
1803: Dissolved and amalgamated into the 56th Line Regiment.

The 69th Line Infantry Regiment
(Vigier, 1673)
1796: 69eme Demi-Brigade d'Infanterie de Ligne.
1803: 69eme Régiment d'Infanterie de Ligne.

1805–1807: With the 6th Corps of the Grande Armée *(Gunzburg; Elchingen; Ulm; Scharnitz; Jena; Guttstadt; Passarge; Friedland)*.
1808–1814: In Spain *(Burgos; Corruna; Busaco; Fuentes d'Onoro; Arapiles; Salamanca)*.
1814: *(Orthez; Toulouse)*.
1815: With the Armée du Nord *(Ligny; Paris)*.

The 70th Line Infantry Regiment
(Medoc, 1674)
1796: 70eme Demi-Brigade d'Infanterie de Ligne.
1803: 70eme Régiment d'Infanterie de Ligne.
1807–1812: In Spain and Portugal *(Rorissa; Vimiero; Saragossa; 2nd siege of Saragossa; Corruna; Braga; Oporto; Puente-d'Alconeta; Busaco; Torres Vedras; Sabugal; Arapiles; Cubiry)*.
1813: With the Grande Armée *(Lützen; Bautzen; Leipzig)*.
1814: In France *(La Rothière; Laon)*.
1815: Part of the Armée du Nord *(Fleurus; Wavre)*.

The 71st Line Infantry Regiment
(Vivarais, 1674)
1796: 71eme Demi-Brigade d'Infanterie de Ligne.
1803: Dissolved, the 1st & 2nd battalions joined the 35th, the 3rd battalion the 86th.

The 72nd Line Infantry Regiment
(Vexin, 1674)
1796: 72eme Demi-Brigade d'Infanterie de Ligne.
1803: 72eme Régiment d'Infanterie de Ligne.
1805–1806: Part of the Armée du Nord.
1806–1808: With the reserve corps of the Grande Armée *(Friedland)*.
1809: Part of the Armées du Rhin et d'Allemagne *(Thann; Essling; Wagram)*.
1812: Part of the 3rd Corps of the Grande Armée *(Moskowa)*.
1813: Part of the 2nd Corps of the Grande Armée *(Kulm; Leipzig)*.
1814: With the 2eme Corps d'Armée *(Laon)*.
1815: Part of the Armée du Nord *(Quatre-Bras; Waterloo)*.

The 73rd Line Infantry Regiment
(Royal-Comtois, 1674)
1796: 73eme Demi-Brigade d'Infanterie de Ligne.
1803: Disbanded and incorporated into the 23rd Line Regiment.

The 74th Line Infantry Regiment
(Beaujolais, 1674)
1796: 74eme Demi-Brigade d'Infanterie de Ligne.
1803: Disbanded.

The 75th Line Infantry Regiment
(Monsieur, 1674)
1796: 75eme Demi-Brigade d'Infanterie de Ligne.
1803: 75eme Régiment d'Infanterie de Ligne.
1805–1807: With the Grande Armée *(Ulm; Memmingen; Austerlitz; Jena; Hoff; Eylau; Heilsberg; Danzig)*.

1808–1813: In Spain *(Talavera; Ocana; Albuhera; Almonacid)*.

1814: In France *(Orthez; Toulouse)*.

1815: Part of the Armée du Nord *(Fleurus; Quatre-Bras; Gembloux; Namur)*.

The 76th Line Infantry Regiment
(Chateauvieux, 1677)

1796: 76eme Demi-Brigade d'Infanterie de Ligne.

1803: 76eme Régiment d'Infanterie de Ligne.

1805–1807: With the Grande Armée *(Elchingen; Ulm; Jena; Friedland)*.

1809: The 1st battalion with the Grande Armée at *(Essling; Wagram)*.

1808–1809: Part of the Armées d'Espagne et de Portugal *(Tamames; Ciudad-Rodrigo)*.

1811–1812: *(Les Arapiles)*.

1813–1814: *(Col de Maya; Pampelune; Bayonne; Orthez; Toulouse)*.

1813: Some battalions took part in the Saxon campaign *(Defence of Dresden)*.

1815: Part of the Armée du Nord *(Fleurus; Wavre)*.

The 77th Line Infantry Regiment
(La Marck, 1680)

1796: 77eme Demi-Brigade d'Infanterie de Ligne.

1803: Disbanded.

The 78th Line Infantry Regiment
(Penthièvre, 1684)

1796: 78eme Demi-Brigade d'Infanterie de Ligne.

1803: Incorporated into the 2nd Line Regiment.

The 79th Line Infantry Regiment
(Boulonnais, 1684)

1796: 79eme Demi-Brigade d'Infanterie de Ligne.

1803: 79eme Régiment d'Infanterie de Ligne.

1805: Part of the Armée d'Italie *(Caldiero)*.

1806–1809: Took part in the Dalmatian campaign *(Gospich; siege of Raguse; Castel-Nuovo; Wagram)*.

1810: Part of the Armée de Naples.

1810–1814: With the Armée de Catalogne.

The 80th Line Infantry Regiment
(Angoumois, 1684)

1796: 80eme Demi-Brigade d'Infanterie de Ligne.

1803: Incorporated into the 34th Line Regiment.

The 81st Line Infantry Regiment
(Conti, 1684)

1796: 81eme Demi-Brigade d'Infanterie de Ligne.

1803: 81eme Régiment d'Infanterie de Ligne.

1805: Part of the Grande Armée *(Hollabruenn)*.

1806–1809: In Dalmatia *(Raguse; Gospich; Wagram)*.

1810–1814: In Spain *(Juesca; Toulouse)*.

The 82nd Line Infantry Regiment
(Saintonge, 1684)

1799: 82eme Demi-Brigade d'Infanterie de Ligne.

1803: 82eme Régiment d'Infanterie de Ligne.
1803–1809: Stationed in Guadeloupa and Martinique.
1807–1814: In Portugal and Spain *(Vimiero; Ciudad-Rodrigo; Almeida; Busaco; Torres Vedras; Fuentes d'Onoro; Salamanca; Bayonne).*
1813: Some battalions with the 6th Corps of the Grande Armée *(Lützen; Bautzen; Jauer; Leipzig; Mayence).*
1814: In France *(Montereau; Sardun; Sommepuis; St Dizier).*
1815: Part of the 2nd Corps during the '100 days' *(Ligny).*

The 83rd Line Infantry Regiment
(Foix, 1684)
1796: 83eme Demi-Brigade d'Infanterie de Ligne.
1803: Incorporated into the 3rd Line Regiment.

The 84th Line Infantry Regiment
(Rohan, 1684)
1796: 84eme Demi-Brigade d'Infanterie de Ligne.
1803: 84eme Régiment d'Infanterie de Ligne.
1805: Part of the 2nd Corps of the Grande Armée *(Ulm; Austerlitz).*
1806–1809: Stationed in Italy.
1809: Part of the Armée d'Italie *(Sacile; Prewald; Graetz, Wagram).*
1810–1811: With the Corps d'Observation d'Italie.
1812: Part of the 4th Corps of the Grande Armée *(Ostrowa; Smolensk; Moskowa; Malojaroslawetz; Krasnoe; Berezina).*
1813–1814: In Italy, part of the Corps d'Observation de l'Adige.
1815: With the Armée du Nord *(Fleurus; Waterloo).*

The 85th Line Infantry Regiment
(Diesbach, 1690)
1796: 85eme Demi-Brigade d'Infanterie de Ligne.
1803: 85eme Régiment d'Infanterie de Ligne.
1805: With the Grande Armée at *(Ulm).*
1806–1808: Still with the Grande Armée *(Auerstaedt; Custrin; Pultusk; Eylau).*
1809–1810: Part of the Armées d'Allemagne et du Rhin *(Eckmuehl; Ratisbonne; Wagram).*
1812–1813: With the Grande Armée *(Mohilow; Moskowa; Moscow; Pirna; Kulm; Dresden).*
1814: In France *(Laon).*
1815: With the Armée du Nord at *(Waterloo).*

The 86th Line Infantry Regiment
(Courten; 1689)
1796: 86eme Demi-Brigade d'Infanterie de Ligne.
1803: 86eme Régiment d'Infanterie de Ligne.
1805: Part of the Armée des Côtes de l'Océan.
1808–1814: With the Armée de Portugal *(Villaviciosa; Evora; Vimiero; Oporto; Amarante; Palor; Arapiles; Orthez; Toulouse).*
1813–1814: With the Grande Armée *(Lützen; Bautzen; Dresden; Moeckern; Leipzig; Hanau; Ockheim; siege of Mayence; Valjouan; Montereau; Laubressel).*
1815: Part of the Armée du Nord *(Ligny; Namur).*

The 87th Line Infantry Regiment
(Dillon, 1690)
1799: 87eme Demi-Brigade d'Infanterie de Ligne.
1803: Incorporated into the 5th Line Regiment.

The 88th Line Infantry Regiment
(Berwick, 1698)
1796: 88eme Demi-Brigade d'Infanterie de Ligne.
1803: 88eme Régiment d'Infanterie de Ligne.
1805: Part of the 5th Corps of the Grande Armée *(Ulm; Hollabruenn; Austerlitz)*.
1806–1807: Still with the 5th Corps *(Jena; Pultusk)*.
1809: The 4th battalion was with the 2nd Corps of the Grande Armée *(Ebersberg; Essling; Wagram)*.
1809–1814: In Spain *(Ocana; Gebora; Badajoz; Albufera; Vittoria)*.
1814: In France *(Laon; Paris)*.
1815: *(Ligny; Wavre)*.

The 89th Line Infantry Regiment
(Royal-Suédois, 1690)
1796: 89eme Demi-Brigade d'Infanterie de Ligne.
1803: Dissolved.

The 90th Line Infantry Regiment
(Chartres, 1691)
1798: 90eme Demi-Brigade d'Infanterie de Ligne.
1803: Incorporated into the 93rd Line Regiment.

The 91st Line Infantry Regiment
(Barrois, 1692)
1799: 91eme Demi-Brigade d'Infanterie de Ligne.
1803: Incorporated into the 20th Line Regiment.

The 92nd Line Infantry Regiment
(Walsh, 1698)
1796: 92eme Demi-Brigade d'Infanterie de Ligne.
1803: 92eme Régiment d'Infanterie de Ligne.
1805: With the Grande Armée at *(Ulm)*.
1809: Part of the Armée d'Italie *(Sacile; Piave; Isonzo; Gratz; Wagram; Tyrolean expedition)*.
1812–1813: With the Grande Armée *(Moskowa; Malojaroslawetz; Wiasma; Krasnoe; Glogau)*.
1813: Part of the 2eme Corps d'Observation d'Italie *(Feistritz; Kraimburg; Bassano; Caldiero)*.
1814: With the Armée d'Italie *(Mincio; Parma; Reggio)*.
1815: Part of the Armée du Nord *(Ligny; Quatre-Bras; Waterloo)*.

The 93rd Line Infantry Regiment
(Enghien, 1706)
1796: 93eme Demi-Brigade d'Infanterie de Ligne.
1803: 93eme Régiment d'Infanterie de Ligne.
1803–1806: Naval Service *(Trafalgar)*.
1807: With the Grande Armée *(siege of Colberg)*.
1808: Part of the Armée d'Espagne.

1809: Part of the 4th Corps of the Armée d'Allemagne *(Eckmuehl; Essling; Wagram; Klagenfurth).*

1810: Part of the Corps d'Observation de la Hollande.

1811: With the Armée de Catalogne.

1812–1814: With the 3rd Corps of the Grande Armée *(Smolensk; Valouttina; Moskowa; Krasnoe; Berezina; Dresden; Leipzig; Magdebourg).*

1815: With the Armée du Nord at *(Waterloo).*

The 94th Line Infantry Regiment
(Royal-Hesse-Darmstadt, 1709)

1796: 94eme Demi-Brigade d'Infanterie de Ligne.

1803: 94eme Régiment d'Infanterie de Ligne.

1805–1807: Part of the 1st Corps of the Grande Armée *(Austerlitz; Lübeck; Mohrungen; Ostrolenka; Friedland).*

1809–1810: With the Armée d'Allemagne *(Essling; Wagram).*

1808–1813: With the Armées d'Espagne et de Portugal *(Espinosa; Alcala; Almeida).*

1813: *(Dresden; defence of Danzig).*

1814: French campaign *(defence of Bayonne).*

The 95th Line Infantry Regiment
(Salis-Grisons, 1734)

1798: 95eme Demi-Brigade d'Infanterie de Ligne.

1803: 95eme Régiment d'Infanterie de Ligne.

1805–1807: With the 1st Corps of the Grande Armée *(Austerlitz; Schleitz; Lubeck; Friedland).*

1809: Part of the Armée d'Allemagne *(Essling; Wagram).*

1811: With the Armée de Portugal.

1808–1814: Part of the Armée d'Espagne, excepting for 1811 *(Durango; Espinosa; Uclés; Medellin; Cadix).*

1813: *(Danzig).*

1815: *(Ligny; Waterloo).*

The 96th Line Infantry Regiment
(Nassau, 1745)

1796: 96eme Demi-Brigade d'Infanterie de Ligne.

1803: 96eme Régiment d'Infanterie de Ligne.

1804–1805: Part of the Armée des Côtes de l'Océan.

1805–1807: With the 6th Corps of the Grande Armée: *(Albeck; Haslach; Diernstein).*
With the 1st Corps of the Grande Armée *(Halle; Braunsberg; Friedland).*

1807–1808: With the Corps d'Occupation de Prusse.

1808–1813: Part of the Armée d'Espagne.

1813: With the Grande Armée.

1813–1814: With the Armée des Pyrennés *(Toulouse).*

1815: *(Ligny; Namur; Villers-Cotterets; Issy).*

The 97th Line Infantry Regiment
(Steiner, 1752)

1796: 97eme Demi-Brigade d'Infanterie de Ligne.

1803: Incorporated into the 60th Line Regiment.

The 98th Line Infantry Regiment
(Bouillon, 1757)
1799: 98eme Demi-Brigade d'Infanterie de Ligne.
1803: Incorporated into the 92nd Line Regiment.

The 99th Line Infantry Regiment
(Royal-Deux-Ponts, 1757)
1796: 99eme Demi-Brigade d'Infanterie de Ligne.
1803: Incorporated into the 62nd Line Regiment.

The 100th Line Infantry Regiment
(Rheinbach, 1758)
1796: 100eme Demi-Brigade d'Infanterie de Ligne.
1803: 100eme Régiment d'Infanterie de Ligne.
1805: With the Grande Armée *(Ulm; Diernstein; Austerlitz)*.
1806–1807: Still with the Grande Armée *(Jena; Eylau; Friedland)*.
1808–1814: In Spain *(Burgos; Saragossa)*.
1815: *(Ligny; Waterloo)*.

The 101st Line Infantry Regiment
(Royal-Liégeois, 1787)
1799: 101eme Demi-Brigade d'Infanterie de Ligne.
1803: 101eme Régiment d'Infanterie de Ligne.
1805: Part of the Armée d'Italie *(passage of the Adigo; Caldiero)*.
1806–1810: Part of the Armée de Naples *(Gaëte)*.
1807–1809: Quelling the Naples revolts.
1809–1810: The Calabrian campaign and the Tyrolean expedition.
1811–1813: Part of the Armées d'Espagne et de Portugal *(Arapiles)*.
1813–1814: Part of the Spanish Armée du Nord *(passage of the Bidassoa; Bayonne)*.
1813: Part of the Grande Armée *(Bautzen; Jueterbock; Leipzig; Hanau)*.
1813–1814: With the Corps d'Observation de l'Adige *(Roverbella)*.
1814: In France *(Bar-sur-Aube; Arcis-sur-Aube)*.
1815: Part of the Armée du Rhin *(defence of Neufbrisach)*.

The 103rd Line Infantry Regiment
1791: 103eme Régiment d'Infanterie de Ligne.
1796: 103eme Demi-Brigade d'Infanterie de Ligne.
1803: 103eme Régiment d'Infanterie de Ligne.
1803–1804: Part of the Armée de Hanovre.
1805–1807: With the Grande Armée *(Ulm; Diernstein; occupation of Vienna; Saalfeld; Jena; occupation of Spandau; Pultusk; Ostrolenka)*.
1808: With the Armée d'Espagne at the *(siege of Saragossa)*.
1809: The 4th battalion served with the Armée d'Allemagne *(Ebersberg; Essling; Wagram)*.
The rest with the Armée d'Espagne *(Talavera; Ocana)*.
1810: The 4th battalion served with the Armée de Portugal.
1811–1812: In Spain *(Badajoz; siege and sacking of Banajoz; Albufera; the Andalusian campaign)*.
1813: *(Vittoria; Col de Maya)*.
1813: Part of the Armée d'Allemagne *(Lützen; Bautzen; Pirna; Kulm; Leipzig; Hanau)*.
1814: With the Armée d'Espagne at *(Toulouse)*.

The 102nd Line Infantry Regiment
1791: 102eme Régiment d'Infanterie de Ligne.
1796: 102eme Demi-Brigade d'Infanterie de Ligne.
1803: 102eme Régiment d'Infanterie de Ligne.
1805: Part of the Armée d'Italie *(passage of the Adigo; Caldiero; Gradisca)*.
1806–1808: With the Armée de Naples *(Rocca-Gloriosa; Fiume-Fredo; Capestrenno; Terriolo; Brancaleone; Capri)*.
1809: Again part of the Armée d'Italie *(Sacile; Soave; Malborghetto; Raab; Wagram)*.
1810–1812: In Spain *(Olot; Ribas)*.
1813–1814: The 1st & 2nd battalions remained in Spain.
1813–1814: The 3rd & 6th battalions served in Italy *(Tarvis; Villach; Bassano)*.
1813–1814: The 4th battalion served with the Grande Armée *(Lützen; Leipzig)*.
1815: With the Corps d'Observation du Jura *(Dannemarie; Valdieu; Belfort)*.

The 104th Line Infantry Regiment
1791: 104eme Régiment d'Infanterie de Ligne.
1799: 104eme Demi-Brigade d'Infanterie de Ligne.
1803: In October, incorporated into the 11th Line Regiment.
1814: Reformed at Mayence with the remnants of the 52nd, 17th and 101st Line Regiments.
1815: *(Defence of Strasbourg; battle on the Suffel)*.

The 105th Line Infantry Regiment
(Le Roi, 1663)
1796: 105eme Demi-Brigade d'Infanterie de Ligne.
1803: 105eme Régiment d'Infanterie de Ligne.
1805: Part of the 7th Corps of the Grande Armée *(Operations in Varalberg; Embs)*.
1806: With the Grande Armée at *(Jena)*.
1806–1807: Part of the 7th, then 4th Corps of the Grande Armée *(Kolozomb; Golymin; Eylau; Heilsberg)*.
1809: With the Armée d'Allemagne *(Ratisbonne; Eckmuehl; Essling; Wagram)*.
1811–1813: In Spain *(Castro; Tolosa; Bidassoa; Saint-Pierre)*.
1812–1814: In Russia and Germany *(Wittemberg; Hamburg; operations in Mecklembourg; siege of Hamburg)*.
1814: In France *(Bar-sur-Aube; Arcis-sur-Aube; St Dizier)*.
1815: *(Waterloo)*.

The 106th Line Infantry Regiment
(Régiment du Cap, 1772)
1796: 106eme Demi-Brigade d'Infanterie de Ligne.
1803: 106eme Régiment d'Infanterie de Ligne.
1805–1810: Part of the Armée d'Italie *(passage of the Adigo; Sacile; Raab; Wagram)*.
1812: With the 4th Corps of the Grande Armée *(Ostrowno, Moskowa; Malojaroslawetz)*.
1813–1814: In Italy *(Castagnaro; Barghetto; Plaisance)*.

The 107th Line Infantry Regiment
(Régiment de Pondichéry, 1772)
1798: 107eme Demi-Brigade d'Infanterie de Ligne.
1803: Dissolved.
1814: Reformed with battalions from the 6th, 10th, 20th and 102nd Line
Regiments.
1814: *(La Chausse; Châlons; Ferté-sous-Jouarre)*.
1815: *(Ligny; Waterloo)*.

The 108th Line Infantry Regiment
(Régiment de l'Isle-de-France, 1772)
1796: 108eme Demi-Brigade d'Infanterie de Ligne.
1803: 108eme Régiment d'Infanterie de Ligne.
1805–1807: With the Grande Armée *(Mariazell; Austerlitz; Auerstaedt;*
Eylau).
1809: With the Armée d'Allemagne *(Thann)*.
1812: With the Grande Armée in Russia *(Mohilow; Moskowa; Krasnoe;*
Berezina).
1813–1814: Part of the 13th Corps of the Grande Armée *(defence of*
Hamburg and Anvers).
1815: With the Armée du Nord *(Ligny; Waterloo)*.

The 109th Line Infantry Regiment
(Régiment de la Martinique et de la Guadeloupe, 1772)
1796: 109eme Demi-Brigade d'Infanterie de Ligne.
1803: Incorporated into the 21st Line Regiment.

The 110th Line Infantry Regiment
(Régiment du Port-au-Prince, 1773)
1799: 110eme Demi-Brigade d'Infanterie de Ligne.
1803: The 1st battalion was incorporated into the 55th Line Regiment; the
2nd & 3rd into the 86th Line Regiment.

The 111th Line Infantry Regiment
1793: 111eme Régiment d'Infanterie de Ligne.
1802: 111eme Demi-Brigade d'Infanterie de Ligne.
1803: 111eme Régiment d'Infanterie de Ligne.
1805–1807: Part of the Grande Armée *(Austerlitz; Auerstaedt; Nasielk;*
Lipucki; Mizinieck; Ostrolenka; Guttstadt; Heilberg; Koenigs-
berg; Friedland).
1809: With the Armée d'Allemagne *(Ambach; Amberg; Tengen; Landshut;*
Eckmuehl; Ratisbonne; Essling; Wagram).
1812: Rejoins the Grande Armée *(Mohilow; Smolensk; Wiasma; Schwar-*
dino; Moskowa; Mojaïsk; Malojaroslawetz; Kolskoï; Wiasma;
Krasnoe).
1813: *(Defence of Stettin and Hamburg; Modlin)*.
1815: *(Ligny; Wavre; Rixensart)*.

The 112th Line Infantry Regiment
1794: 112eme Demi-Brigade de Bataille.
1801: 112eme Demi-Brigade d'Infanterie de Ligne.
1803: 112eme Régiment d'Infanterie de Ligne.
1807–1809: Part of the 3rd Division de Réserve of the Armée d'Italie.
(Volano; Col de Tarvis; Raab; Wagram).

1808–1811: The 4th battalion served with the Armée de Catalogne *(La Fluvia; Cardedeu; Molins-del-Rey; Valls)*.

1813: Part of the 11th Corps of the Grande Armée *(Mersebourg; Bautzen; Loewenberg; Goldberg; Katzbach; Leizig; Hanau)*.

1813–1814: With the Armée d'Italie.

The 113th Line Infantry Regiment

1795: 113eme Demi-Brigade de Bataille.

1796: Dissolved and incorporated into the 85eme Demi-Brigade.

1808: Reformed.

1811–1812: With the Armée d'Espagne.
Catalonian campaign *(Gerona; siege of Rosas)*.
The 1st & 2nd battalions *(Bonas; Aldéa-del-Ponte; Ciudad Rodrigo)*.

1812: The 3rd & 4th battalions served in Russia and formed part of the rear-guard of the Grande Armée from Wilna.

1813–1814: *(Defence of Danzig and Wurtzbourg)*.

1814: In France *(Champaubert; Paris)*.

1814: Dissolved into the 4th, 14th & 72nd Line Regiments.

The 114th Line Infantry Regiment

1795: 114eme Demi-Brigade de Bataille.

1798: Incorporated into the 35eme Demi-Brigade d'Infanterie.

1808: Reformed as the 114th.

1808–1814: In Spain *(Medina-del-Rio; Tudela; siege of Saragossa; Alcaniz; Maria; Belchite; Lerida; Las Curvas; Uldecona; Tortose; Mont-serrat; Sagonte; Valencia; Peniscola; Villena; Castella; defence of Sagonte; defence of Tortose; defence of Pampelune)*.

The 115th Line Infantry Regiment

1808: 115eme Régiment d'Infanterie de Ligne.

1808–1811: Part of the 3rd Corps of the Armée d'Espagne *(The Madrid insurrection; the Valencian expedition; Tudela; Saragossa; Maria; Belchite; Lerida; Tortose; Andora)*.

1811: With the Armée d'Aragon at *(Tarragona)*.

1811–1813: Part of the Armée de Catalogne *(Altafulla; Molins-del-Rey; La Salud; St Privat)*.

1813–1814: With the Armées des Pyrennés, du Midi et de Lyon *(Cubiry; Irun; Garris; Orthez; Lyon; Toulouse)*.

The 116th Line Infantry Regiment

1794: 116eme Demi-Brigade de Bataille.

1796: Incorporated into the 84eme Demi-Brigade d'Infanterie.

1808: Reformed as the 116th.

1808–1814: In Spain *(Baylen; Tudela; Saragossa; Lerida; Tivisa; Tortose; Taragona; Sagonte; Valencia; Castalla; Yécla; Ordal; Tarbes; Toulouse)*.

The 117th Line Infantry Regiment

1794: 117eme Demi-Brigade de Bataille.

1796: Incorporated into the 75eme Demi-Brigade d'Infanterie.

1808: Reformed as the 117th.

1808–1814: In Spain *(Tudela; siege of Saragossa; Alfarras; Lerida; siege of Tortose; Tarragona; Sagonte; Col de San Antonio; siege of Valencia; defence of Pampelune; defence of Barcelona and Eastern Pyrennés; Toulouse).*

The 118th Line Infantry Regiment
1794: 118eme Demi-Brigade de Bataille.
1796: Incorporated into the 32eme Demi-Brigade d'Infanterie.
1808: Reformed as the 118th.
1808–1814: In Spain *(Aquilar-del-Campo; El Padron; St Martin-de-Miranda; Arapiles; Vittoria; Bidassoa; Nive; Orthez; Toulouse).*
1814: The 6th battalion served with the Grande Armée at *(Arcis-sur-Aube).*

The 119th Line Infantry Regiment
1808: 119eme Régiment d'Infanterie de Ligne.
1808–1814: The Spanish campaign *(Medina-del-Rio-Seco; Burgos; Saragossa; occupation of Asturia; Santander; Quintanilla; Salamanca; Arapiles; Vittoria; Bidassoa; Bayonne; Orthez; Toulouse).*

The 120th Line Infantry Regiment
1808: 120eme Régiment d'Infanterie de Ligne.
1808–1814: With the Armée d'Espagne *(Medina-del-Rio-Seco; Selis; Pisnas; Congas-Desnas; Grado; Santillana; Santander; Penaflor; bridge of the Cornillana; Tabergo; Fresnoe; Puelo; Ostera de las Duenas; Arapiles; Vittoria; Bridge of Irun; Bayonne; Orthez: Toulouse).*

The 121st Line Infantry Regiment
1794: 121eme Demi-Brigade de Bataille.
1796: Incorporated into the 39eme Demi-Brigade d'Infanterie.
1809: Reformed as the 121st.
1809–1813: Part of the Armée d'Espagne *(siege of Saragossa; San Juan-de-la-Pena; Tarriente; Lerida; Alventosa; Fuente-Santa; Blancas; Checa; Penas; siege of Tarragona; siege of Valencia; Yecla; Biar; Castella; San Felice).*
1813: With the Grande Armée *(Lützen; Bautzen; Würschen; Dresden; Leipzig).*
1814: In France *(Rosnay; Arcis-sur-Aube; Paris).*

The 122nd Line Infantry Regiment
1794: 122eme Demi-Brigade de Bataille.
1796: Incorporated into the 57eme Demi-Brigade d'Infanterie.
1809: Reformed as the 122nd.
1809–1810: Part of the 2nd Corps of the Armée d'Espagne *(Corruna; Ferrol; Lahonzo; Oporto; Infestio; Puente los Fieros).*
1811–1813: Bonnet's Division of the 6th Corps of the Armée d'Espagne *(Quintanilla-del-Valle; Arapiles; Estepar; Osmo; Subijana de Morillas; Vittoria; Pampelune; Bidassoa).*
1813–1814: The 4th, then the 7th Corps of the Grande Armée in Germany *(Lützen; Würschen; Falkenheim; Zinwald; Moeckern; Leipzig; Hocheim).*

1814: In France the battalions were distributed throughout the 1st, 4th, 6th, 7th and Ney's army corps *(Nogent; Valjouan; Montereau; Mery; Fontvannes; Bar-sur-Aube; Craonne; Laon; Arcis-sur-Aube; Saint Dizier)*.

The 123rd Line Infantry Regiment
1793: 123eme Demi-Brigade de Bataille.
1796: Incorporated into the 99eme Demi-Brigade d'Infanterie.
1810: Reformed with Dutch troops, as the 123rd.
1812: Part of the 2nd Corps of the Grande Armée *(Polotsk; Tchaniski; Berezina)*.
1813–1814: Still with the Grande Armée *(defence of Wittenberg and Wesel)*.

The 124th Line Infantry Regiment
1795: 124eme Demi-Brigade de Bataille.
1796: Incorporated into the 94eme Demi-Brigade d'Infanterie.
1810: Reformed as the 124th with Dutch troops.
1810: Part of the Corps d'Observation de la Hollande.
1811: With the Corps d'Observation de l'Océan.
1812: With the Corps d'Observation de l'Elbe.
1812: Formed part of Verdier's Division of Oudinot's 2nd Corps: *(passage of the Niemen at Kowno; Deweltowo; Oboiardszina; Polotsk; Tchaniski; Borisow; Berezina; Kowno)*.
1813: *(Siege of Stettin)*.
1814: *(Sieges of Wittenberg and Wesel)*.
    In May, incorporated into the 25th Line Regiment.

The 125th Line Infantry Regiment
1795: 125eme Demi-Brigade de Bataille.
1796: Incorporated into the 34eme Demi-Brigade d'Infanterie.
1810: Reformed, with Dutch troops, as the 125th.
1811: Part of the Armée de Hollande.
1812: With the 9th Corps of the Grande Armée *(Smoliany; Borisow; Berezina)*.
1813: The regiment was dissolved.

The 126th Line Infantry Regiment
1795: 126eme Demi-Brigade de Bataille.
1810: Reformed as the 126th.
1811: Part of the Corps d'Observation du Rhin.
1812: At the camp de Boulogne and with the 9th Corps of the Grande Armée *(Smoliany; Borisow; Berezina)*.
1813: Incorporated into the 123rd Line Regiment.

The 127th Line Infantry Regiment
1794: 127eme Demi-Brigade de Bataille.
1796: Incorporated into the 3eme Demi-Brigade d'Infanterie.
1811: Reformed as the 127th.
1811: Part of Davout's Corps de l'Elbe in garrison in Hamburg and Luxemburg.
1812: In Russia *(Smolensk; Valoutina; Moskowa; Malojaroslawetz; Wiasma; Berezina)*.
1814: Defence of *(Wesel)*.

The 128th Line Infantry Regiment
1794: 128eme Demi-Brigade de Bataille.
1796: Incorporated into the 7eme Demi-Brigade d'Infanterie.
1811: Reformed as the 128th.
1811: Part of the Corps d'Observation de l'Elbe.
1812: With the 2nd Corps of the Grande Armée *(Jacobowo; Drissa; Polotsk; Smoliany; Borisow; Berezina)*.
1813: *(Defence of Custrin and Wurtzburg)*.
1814: *(Defence of Kehl)*.
1814: Incorporated in May into the 40th and 53rd Line Regiments.

The 129th Line Infantry Regiment
1793: 129eme Demi-Brigade de Bataille.
1796: Absorbed into the 32eme Demi-Brigade d' Infanterie.
1811: Recreated as the 129th.
1812: The 1st & 2nd battalions served in Russia *(Krasnoe; Berezina; Kowno)*.
1813: The 3rd battalion took part in the *(siege of Spandau)*.
1813: Dissolved and incorporated into the 127th & 128th Line Regiments.

The 130th Line Infantry Regiment
1795: 130eme Demi-Brigade de Bataille.
1796: Incorporated into the 4eme Demi-Brigade d'Infanterie.
1811: Reformed as the 130th.
1811–1813: In Spain *(Santander; Cabezon-del-Sal; Torrelavega; Tejo; Burgos; Santona; Pampelune; Sarre; Bayonne)*.
1814: In France *(Montmirail; Bar-sur-Aube; L'Echelle; Arcis-sur-Aube)*.

The 131st Line Infantry Regiment
1794: 131eme Demi-Brigade de Bataille.
1796: Became the 1er Demi-Brigade d'Infanterie de Ligne.
1811: Became the Régiment de Walcheren.
1812: In Russia *(defence of the Wolkowisk bridge)*.
1812: Renamed the 131eme Régiment d'Infanterie de Ligne.
1813: In Russia *(Kalisch)*.
1813: Part of the Grande Armée *(Lützen, Bautzen; Reichenbach; Grossbeeren; Dennewitz; Leipzig; Hanau)*.
1814: In France *(defence of Metz)*.
1813–1814: The 2nd battalion served in Italy *(Saffnitz; Mincio)*.

The 132nd Line Infantry Regiment
1794: 132eme Demi-Brigade de Bataille.
1796: Absorbed into the 108eme Demi-Brigade d'Infanterie.
1811: Became the Régiment de l'Isle-de-Ré.
1812: Renamed the 132eme Régiment d'Infanterie de Ligne.
1812–1813: In Russia *(Wolkowisk; Kalisch)*.
1813: With the Grande Armée *(Bautzen; Wittstock; Grossbeeren; Dennewitz; Roslau; Leipzig; Freyburg; Hanau)*.
1813: Part of the 2nd battalion of the Armée d'Italie *(Villach; Caldiero; Ferrare)*.
1814: In France *(St Dizier; La Rothière; Rosnay; Champaubert; Vauchamps; Meaux; May-en-Multier; Neuilly-St Front; Laon; Reims; Berry-au-Bac; Fère-Champenoise; Paris)*.
1814: The 4th battalion in Italy *(Mincio; Parma)*.

The 133rd Line Infantry Regiment
1811: Created as the 2eme Régiment de la Méditerranée.
1812: Renamed as the 133eme Régiment d'Infanterie de Ligne.
1812–1813: In Russia *(Wolkowisk; Kalisch)*.
1813: With the Grande Armée *(Bautzen; Grossbeeren; Dennewitz; Leipzig; Hanau)*.
1813–1814: *(Defence of Modlin, Landau and Torgau)*.

The 134th Line Infantry Regiment
1795: 134eme Demi-Brigade de Bataille.
1796: Incorporated into the 70eme Demi-Brigade d'Infanterie.
1813: Reformed as the 134th with troops of the Garde de Paris.
1813: Part of the Grande Armée *(Moeckern; Lützen; Bautzen; Loewenberg; action on the Bober)*.
1814: *(Defence of Magdebourg)*.

The 135th Line Infantry Regiment
1813: Formed of battalions of National Guard as 135th.
1813: Part of the 5th Corps of the Grande Armée *(Lützen; Weissig; Lowenberg; Goldberg; Leipzig; Hanau)*.
1814: With the 2nd, then the 11th Corps of the Grande Armée *(Mormant; Montereau; Bar-sur-Aube; Romainville plateau)*.

The 136th Line Infantry Regiment
1813: Formed as the 136th with battalions of the National Guard.
1813: With the Grande Armée *(Lützen; Bautzen; Leipzig)*.
1814: In France *(Montmirail; Vauchamps; Meaux; Paris; Sarrelouis; siege of Soissons)*.

The 137th Line Infantry Regiment
1813: Formed as the 137th with battalions of the National Guard.
1813–1814: Part of the 12th Corps of the Grande Armée *(Kaya; Würschen; Hoyerswerda; Dennewitz; Leipzig; Hanau; siege of Torgau; siege of Mayence)*.
1814: *(Defence of Gênes)*.

The 138th Line Infantry Regiment
1794: 138eme Demi-Brigade de Bataille.
1796: Incorporated into the 61eme Demi-Brigade d'Infanterie.
1813: Reformed as the 138th with battalions of the National Guard.
1813: Part of the 3rd Corps of the Grande Armée *(Lützen; Bautzen; Dessau; Leipzig; Hanau)*.
1814: With the 6th Corps of the Grande Armée *(La Rothière; Champaubert; Montmirail; Vauchamps; Paris)*.

The 139th Line Infantry Regiment
1794: 139eme Demi-Brigade de Bataille.
1797: Incorporated into the 21eme Demi-Brigade d'Infanterie. Excepting three companies of grenadiers that were absorbed into the Légion Francs.
1813: Reformed as the 139th with battalions of the National Guard.
1813: Part of the Grande Armée *(Rippach; Lützen; Bautzen; Haynau; Katzbach; Lieberwolkwitz; Wachau; Probstheyda; Leipzig; Hanau)*.
1814: In France *(Châlons-sur-Marne; Château-Thierry; Ferté-sous-Jouarre; St Parre; Arcis-sur-Aube; St Dizier)*.

The 140th Line Infantry Regiment
1794: 140eme Demi-Brigade de Bataille.
1796: Incorporated into the 62eme Demi-Brigade d'Infanterie.
1813: Reformed with National Guard battalions as the 140th.
1813: Part of the 3rd, then the 5th Corps of the Grande Armée *(Lützen; Bautzen; Wachau; Leipzig; Hanau)*.
1814: With the 11th Corps of the Grande Armée *(defence of Juliers)*.

The 141st Line Infantry Regiment
1794. 141eme Demi-Brigade de Bataille.
1796: Incorporated into the 86eme Demi-Brigade d'Infanterie.
1813: Reformed with National Guard battalions as the 141st.
1813: Part of the Grande Armée *(Lützen; Bautzen; Würschen; Leipzig; Hanau)*.
1814: In France *(Paris)*.

The 142nd Line Infantry Regiment
1795: 142eme Demi-Brigade de Bataille.
1796: Incorporated into the 86eme Demi-Brigade d'Infanterie.
1813: Reformed with National Guard battalions as the 142nd.
1813: Part of the Grande Armée *(Lützen; Koenigswartha; Bautzen; Würschen; Dresden; Hanau)*.
1814: In France *(Rosnay; Nogent; Champaubert; Montmirail)*.

The 143rd Line Infantry Regiment
1795: 143eme Demi-Brigade de Bataille.
1796: Incorporated into the 52eme Demi-Brigade d'Infanterie.
1813: Reformed with National Guard battalions as the 143rd.
1813–1814: Part of the Armée d'Espagne *(Ribas; Molins-del-Rey)*.

The 144th Line Infantry Regiment
1794: 144eme Demi-Brigade de Bataille.
1796: Incorporated into the 52eme Demi-Brigade d'Infanterie.
1813: Reformed with National Guard battalions as the 144th.
1813: With Ricard's Division of the 3rd Corps of the Grande Armée *(Lützen; Bautzen; Katzbach; Leipzig; Hanau)*.
1814: With Ricard's Division of the 6th Corps *(La Rothière; defence of the Dienville bridge; Champaubert; Montmirail; Vauchamps; Laon; Reims; Fère-Champenoise; Paris)*.

The 145th Line Infantry Regiment
1795: 145eme Demi-Brigade de Bataille.
1796: Incorporated into the 4eme Demi-Brigade d'Infanterie.
1813: Reformed with National Guard battalions as the 145th.
1813: Part of the Grande Armée *(Moeckern; Lützen; Würschen; Katzbach; Dessau; Leipzig; Hanau)*.
1814: In France *(La Rothière; defence of the Dienville Bridge; Champaubert; Montmirail; Vauchamps)*.
1814: Joined the Armée de Lyon *(St Julien; Limonest)*.

The 146th Line Infantry Regiment
1795: 146eme Demi-Brigade de Bataille.
1796: Incorporated into the 5eme Demi-Brigade d'Infanterie.
1813: Reformed with National Guard battalions as the 146th.

1813: Part of the Grande Armée *(Würschen; Loewenberg; Goldberg)*.
Dissolved the same year.

The 147th Line Infantry Regiment
1793: 147eme Demi-Brigade de Bataille.
1796: Incorporated into the 4eme Demi-Brigade d'Infanterie.
1813: Reformed with National Guard battalions as the 147th.
1813: Part of the 5th Corps of the Grande Armée *(Würschen; Neukirchen; Plagwitz; Goldberg; 2nd battle of Plagwitz)*.
Dissolved the same year and absorbed into the 154th Line Regiment.

The 148th Line Infantry Regiment
1793: 148eme Demi-Brigade de Bataille.
1797: Incorporated into the 34eme Demi-Brigade d'Infanterie.
1813: Reformed with National Guard battalions as the 148th.
1813: With the Grande Armée *(Loewenberg; passage of the Bober; Goldberg)*.
Dissolved same year.

The 149th Line Infantry Regiment
1794: 149eme Demi-Brigade de Bataille.
1796: Incorporated into the 43rd, 83rd and 105th Demi-Brigades d'Infanterie.
1813: Reformed with National Guard battalions as the 149th.
1813: With the Grande Armée *(Bautzen; Loewenberg; Goldberg; Drebnitz)*.
1814: In France *(Fère-Champenoise)*.

The 150th Line Infantry Regiment
1794: 150eme Demi-Brigade de Bataille.
1796: Incorporated into the 21eme Demi-Brigade d'Infanterie.
1813: Reformed with National Guard battalions as the 150th.
1813: With the Grande Armée *(Zobten; Goldberg; Katzbach; Putzkau; Wachau; Leipzig)*.
1814: *(Defence of Maestricht)*.

The 151st Line Infantry Regiment
1813: Created with National Guard battalions as the 151st.
1813: Part of the Grande Armée *(attack on the Wettin and Halle bridges; Lindeneau; Weissig; Würschen; Haynau)*.
1813–1814: *(Siege of Glogau)*.
1814: Took part in the French campaign.

The 152nd Line Infantry Regiment
1794: 152eme Demi-Brigade de Bataille.
1796: Incorporated into the 75eme Demi-Brigade d'Infanterie.
1813: Reformed with National Guard battalions as the 152nd.
1813: Part of the Grande Armée *(Bremerlehe; Lunebourg; Harbourg; Katzbach; Leipzig)*.
1814: In Fance *(defence of Strasbourg and Paris)*.

The 153rd Line Infantry Regiment
1813: Created with National Guard battalions as the 153rd.
1813: With the Grande Armée *(Wettin; Halle; Lindenau; Leipzig; Weissig; Würschen; Haynau-Michelsdorff; Loewenberg; Goldberg; Katzbach; Barna; Wachau; Leipzig; Hanau)*.

The 154th Line Infantry Regiment
1794: 154eme Demi-Brigade de Bataille.
1796: Incorporated into the 10eme Demi-Brigade d'Infanterie Légère.
1813: Reformed with National Guard battalions as the 154th.
1813: Part of the 5th Corps of the Grande Armée *(Moeckern; Danning-Kow; Weissig; Würschen; Loewenberg; Katzbach; Drebnitz; Lieberwolkwitz; Leipzig)*.
1814: Remained in the 5th Corps throughout French campaign.

The 155th Line Infantry Regiment
1813: Created with National Guard battalions as the 155th.
1813: Part of the 5th Corps of the Grande Armée *(Weissig; Würschen; Goldberg; Katzbach; Drebnitz; Lieberwolkwitz; Leipzig; Hanau)*.
1814: Remained in the 5th Corps *(Pagny; Ferté-sous-Jouarre; Orléans)*.

The 156th Line Infantry Regiment
1813: Created with National Guard battalions as the 156th.
1813: The 1st, 2nd & 4th battalions served with the Grande Armée *(Neukirchen; Bautzen; Lukau; Trebbin; Wilmersdorf; Tragun; Denne-witz; Dessau; Koesen; Hoff; Hocheim)*.
1814: With the Armée de Lyon *(Voreppe; Paris)*.

The 157th Line Infantry Regiment
1795: 157eme Demi-Brigade de Bataille.
1796: Incorporated into the 70eme Demi-Brigade d'Infanterie.
Remained vacant until 1887.

The 158th Line Infantry Regiment
Vacant number.

The 159th Line Infantry Regiment
1794: 159eme Demi-Brigade de Bataille.
1796: Incorporated into the 10eme Demi-Brigade d'Infanterie.
Remained vacant until 1887.

The 160th Line Infantry Regiment
A vacant number until 1887.

The 161st Line Infantry Regiment
1794: 161eme Demi-Brigade de Bataille.
1796: 1st & 3rd battalions incorporated into the 9eme Demi-Brigade d'Infanterie, the 2nd battalion into the 73eme Demi-Brigade d'Infanterie.
Remained vacant until 1887.

The 162nd Line Infantry Regiment
1794: 162eme Demi-Brigade de Bataille.
1796: Incorporated into the 103eme Demi-Brigade d'Infanterie.
Remained vacant until 1887.

The 163rd Line Infantry Regiment
1794: 163eme Demi-Brigade de Bataille.
1796: Became the 36eme Demi-Brigade d'Infanterie de Ligne.
The number remained vacant until 1891.

4: Dress and Equipment

The Imperial infantrymen's uniform progressed from a reasonably homogenous style at the start to a vast diversity of garb during their great years between 1806 and 1810. As the Empire dwindled, so did the resources for uniformly equipping them; despite the 1812 regulations, were it not for the vast number of men lost on campaign and the consequent formation of new regiments, standardization would have taken many more years to achieve. Decrees issued in Paris requiring all troops to adopt the new habit-veste was of little import to men in baking Spanish deserts or freezing Russian steppes, assuming they received first the order and secondly the habit-vestes.

The infantry uniform of 1804 bore barely any resemblance to the popular concept of Imperial dress depicted in modern prints and on many model soldiers. They looked far more like the sans-culottes of the Revolutionary Army of Italy, in their long blue coats, ill-fitting trousers and battered bicorns. Plate 1 (page 17) shows in colour the standard coat, the lapels have seven buttons apiece though the coat is in fact done up by a series of hooks and eyes down the middle, the left hand skirt overlaps the right. Under this was worn a fatigue jacket, giving the appearance of a waistcoat.

This outfit was complemented by a felt bicorn hat. This headdress had no practical value, aside from its cheapness, as it gave the wearer no protection against blows or the elements, having two gutters that carefully channelled the rain down on to the wearer's shoulders; needless to say it was soon knocked out of shape and became shabby exceedingly quickly.

As we have seen, by the end of the forced march that began the Bavarian campaign in 1805, the men had become little more than a tattered horde, very far removed from the efficient, well accoutred ranks we might expect of a conquering army. Having no overcoats, many were obliged to strip the dead of Austerlitz to avoid dying of exposure during those winter months. It was not until April 25, 1806, that it was decided to make overcoats regulation issue, though these did not begin to appear until September 1806. With these and captured foreign headgear and cartridge-pouches, the motley mass heaved its ponderous weight towards fresh conquests.

The practicality of the bicorns finally assessed as nil, shakoes, hitherto reserved for Light infantry regiments, were issued to the Line in 1807. Distribution was setting the pace for all ordinances under Napoleon, a very slow and highly erratic business. The 4th Line Infantry Regiment, for example, counted as late as November only 700 shakoes, amid 2,850 bicorns.

The 1807 shako, decreed on February 25, 1806, was made of felt like the bicorn, but was reinforced with a band of leather at the top and bottom. It had a 'V' shaped chevron on both sides, and a sturdy peak; the fit was adjustable by a buckle placed at the back of the lower leather band. On the front below the cockade was a copper plate bearing the regimental number. The shape of this plate followed no specific pattern and the Imperial years were to see many different types, some of which are illustrated overleaf in Fig. 5. Above the cockade was a pom-pon of company colour. Here again there were highly diverse shapes; there were round ones, round flat ones and carrot shaped ones, all varying in volume. The shako was further embellished for important occasions with cords and tassels. Voltigeurs and grenadiers had their own peculiarities and we shall be dealing with these at length later.

This same year brought another innovation to the already heterogeneous regiments, for Great Britain's Continental Blockade entailed a scarcity of the indigo based dyes used to colour the coat fabric. Infantry coats were consequently to be made of white cloth and an elaborate system was devised to make each regiment readily distinguishable by the facing colours. Previously, the sole means of identifying a particular regiment was by the number on the shako plate and on the buttons.

Essentially, every eight regiments would have a distinctive colour:

1st to 8th Regiments:	Imperial green
9th to 16th Regiments:	Plush black
17th to 24th Regiments:	Scarlet
25th to 32nd Regiments:	Capucine
33rd to 40th Regiments:	Violet
41st to 48th Regiments:	Sky blue
49th to 56th Regiments:	Pink
57th to 64th Regiments:	Golden yellow
65th to 72nd Regiments:	Dark blue
73rd to 80th Regiments:	Jonquil
81st to 88th Regiments:	Grass green
89th to 104th Regiments:	Madder red
105th to 112th Regiments:	Steel grey

Of every series of eight regiments, the first four would have copper buttons and horizontal pockets, the remaining four would have white metal buttons and vertical pockets. Of each half series, the particular colour was used on the following parts of the coat:

First regiment:	On the collar, turnbacks and cuffs.
Second regiment:	On the turnbacks and cuffs.
Third regiment:	On the turnbacks and collar.
Fourth regiment:	On the collar and cuffs.

Thus each regiment was immediately recognisable by the placement of the colour and the direction of the pocket, up to a considerable distance. Where a collar, turnback or cuff remained white, it was piped in the distinctive regimental colour.

This scheme was never fully realised for, in the course of the Polish campaign it became apparent that the coats were almost impossible to keep clean and that the smallest wound appeared appalling, the blood-stain contrasting so vividly with the white cloth. Thus the issue was ceased. The following regiments are known to have been equipped with the new coats but upon wearing out the coats were replaced with the

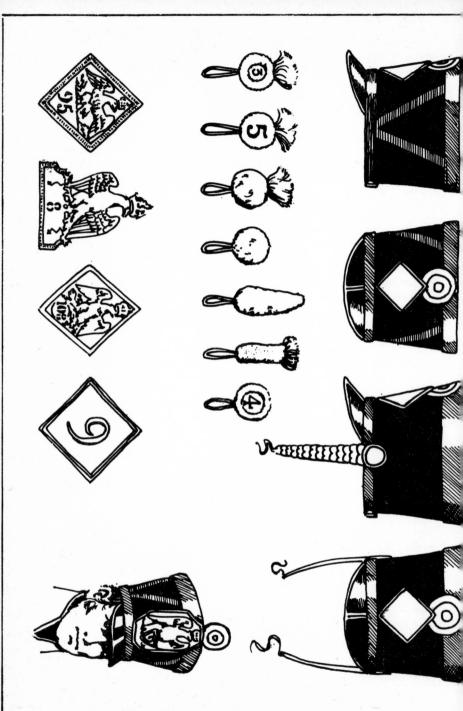

usual blue ones: 3rd, 13th, 14th, 15th, 16th, 17th, 18th, 21st, 32nd, 33rd, 46th and 53rd.

These old-fashioned uniforms were acknowledged as being unfit for the rigours of campaigning. Perfect as they were for spectacular parades, they were very uncomfortable for long drawn out campaigns of mobility. There was much confusion as the wars progressed, not only because of the partial issue of the white coat and the shako, but also because the men would also wear whatever clothes they could find whenever there was an opportunity.

The regulation greatcoat ended 32 centimetres from the ground, and was manufactured in ochre, grey and beige cloth. It could be single or double breasted, with copper or cloth covered buttons, or alternatively toggles.

Trousers were supposed to be of white cloth, but, as they wore out, they were replaced or patched with whatever was at hand. Thus we see infantrymen in blue, brown or grey pairs, varying from tapered to baggy style in cut.

Many foreign items of equipment and dress were assimilated by the capture of enemy depots. Lanne's divisions became the proud possessors of 4,000 Russian style greatcoats in 1806, while Davout's men found themselves with 2,000 pairs of Prussian suede breeches. Small arms and the like were generally pillaged from battlefields if units had deficient stocks.

In 1810 a new model of shako was devised, to be distributed from the beginning of 1811. This is shown lower right in Fig. 5. It was more bell-topped and slightly higher than the 1806 model. It was equipped with a leather upper and lower band and folded within the hat when not in use. The regimental plates became slowly more uniform, either a diamond shape or an eagle mounted upon a semi-circle that bore the regimental number; above the cockade was a flat disc denoting the company by colour:

1st: Dark green
2nd: Sky blue
3rd: Golden yellow
4th: Violet

As usual, many units retained pom-pons of all manner of shapes and sizes. Some shakoes bore a pom-pon of battalion colour, surmounted by a disc of company colour, or the reverse. Others had discs with an outer rim of company colour and the battalion number on a white background in the centre. Cords and tassels were prohibited, but units persisted in their use until the end of the Empire.

The shako was usually covered in a waterproof cloth on campaign to protect it from the vagaries of the weather. The cartridge-pouch was also covered, usually in white cloth, left plain, bearing the regimental number, or the following inscription:

.... Regiment d'Infanterie.
.... Bataillon.
.... Compagnie.

The appropriate number was filled in.

The cartridge-pouch was not the only item hung about the men; water bottles and kitchen utensils of every conceivable description burdened them, tangling up the webbing and the long skirts of their coats.

This 18th century garment was the primary focus of attention of the 1812 regulations. It was as outmoded as the bicorn and a new short coatee (the Spencer coat) was issued to replace it. It fastened at the waist and had a much shorter skirt. These new coatees were not issued until 1813 and then only slowly replaced the old model; by Waterloo, however, most infantrymen wore the new Spencer coat.

The first to receive it were probably the 290,000 conscripts of 1813, who were destined to form three-quarters of the new army to replace the thousands left in the snows of Russia. Every one of them under twenty, these youths were to suffer horribly during the coming years. In 1813 they marched beneath no less than three continuous months of rain, with dysentry and typhoid thinning their underfed ranks. Of the 4,856 stationed in Wurtzburg in August of 1813, 1,317 were in hospital. Thousands were later to die of exhaustion and hunger on the roads of Saxony.

Seventeen and eighteen year old boys were to struggle with the ferocity of veterans to save France during 1814, clad in rags and civilian clothing. These scarecrows courageously bore the last infantry uniforms of Napoleon's army.

FUSILIER COMPANIES

Fusilier companies formed the largest mass of the infantry arm. Raw recruits received their first taste of battle within their serried ranks and should they survive were gradually promoted into the élite companies of voltigeurs or grenadiers.

The dress of fusiliers consisted of the dark blue habit illustrated in Plate 1. The turnback devices for fusiliers are the most difficult of all to specify, for they could be blue cloth eagles, regimental numbers, capital 'N's surmounted with crowns, red heart shapes or diamond shapes, even five pointed stars. As often as not, turnback patches would be ignored altogether.

Fig. 6 depicts the small arms and equipment common to fusiliers, and the individual items are described here.

(A) This is the Year IX pattern musket. It was carried by all infantrymen from around 1810 and weighed 4.65 kgs, approximately 10lbs 4oz, and was 1.53 metres long. Previously a similar model, dating back to 1777, was employed in conjunction with the Mk 1 musket of Republican manufacture.

(B) These are the cartridges employed, the paper rolls contain both shot and powder. The calibre averaged around 1.75 cm.

(C) The fusilier cartridge pouch, carrying a maximum of 50 cartridges. The fatigue cap is rolled and strapped to the bottom of the pouch. The strap itself bears a holder for the bayonet scabbard.

(D) The bayonet and scabbard. The blade is 40.6 cm. long, about 1ft 4ins.

(E) (F) Waterbottles were not specifically distributed to the troops, though each man was required to carry one when on campaign. The men therefore improvised with such examples as these, a glass bottle within a protective wicker covering and a brown gourde, and captured metal canteens.

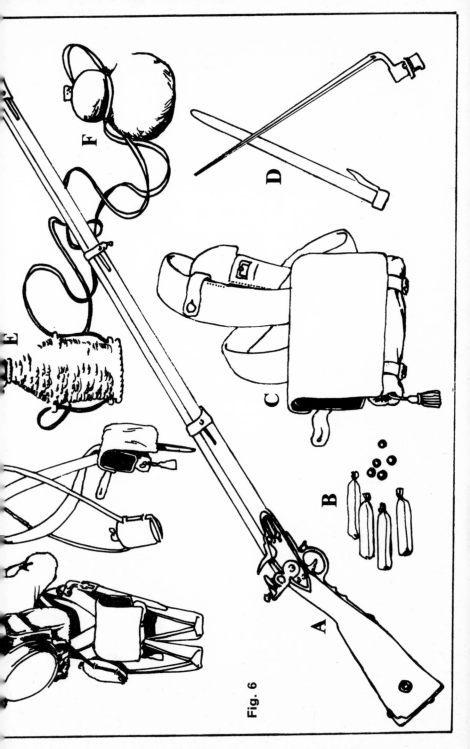

Fig. 6

65

Fig. 7 shows examples of the headgear of the fusilier companies and descriptions are given below:

(A) This is the bicorn hat of the 1801 issue. It bears a spherical pompon of company colour above a tricolour cockade. It is being worn 'en bataille', that is to say crossways on the head as it was positioned for battle.

(B) This is the fatigue cap or 'bonnet de police' of Napoleon's infantry. It is dark blue with red piping and lace. Note the tassel also red, that is hung over the front of the cap.

(C) Once again the 1801 bicorn, this time worn 'en colonne', that is fore and aft, for the march. The cockade is held in position by a strip of yellow lace attached to a tunic button at the bottom. Instead of a spherical pom-pon, he bears the more correct flat disc, edged in wool of the company colour.

(D) The bicorn in profile worn 'en bataille'.

1807–1810

(E) From January of 1807 the bicorn was to be replaced by this model of shako, to better protect the wearer from the elements and cavalry sabres. It has a lower and upper band of leather, also 'V' shaped chevrons on each side. At the back of the lower band is a buckle for adjusting the fit to the individual's requirements. A copper plate was mounted on the front, bearing the regimental number.

(F) The 1807 shako ornamented with white cords and tassels. These were attached solely for special occasions.

(G) The wearer has covered his shako with a cloth cover as might be worn on campaign. Later an oilskin cloth became official issue.

1810–1815

(H) From 1810 this slightly larger and more bell-topped shako was issued. The chevrons have been removed, chin-scales have been added and a leather flap is stitched into the headband. When not in use this was folded inside. In wet weather it was lowered to protect the ears and back of the neck (see also J).

(I) The same shako model, but with cords and tassels added, despite orders to the contrary. Note the chin-straps tied around the pom-pon when not being used.

(J) His 'couvre-nuque' lowered and tied under his chin, and with the shako covered in waterproof fabric, this fusilier protects himself and his head-dress from the elements.

Officers

(K) From 1801 until the introduction of the shako, officers were equipped with bicorns similar to those of the rank and file. Many officers added golden tassels to both ends. After 1806, the bicorn was not discarded, but reserved for off duty wear and the march.

(L) An alternative to wearing the bicorn in undress was this fatigue cap. It is identical to the pattern of the rank and file but with golden piping, lace and tassel.

(M) Here is the officers' model of the 1807 shako. The only difference

Fig. 7

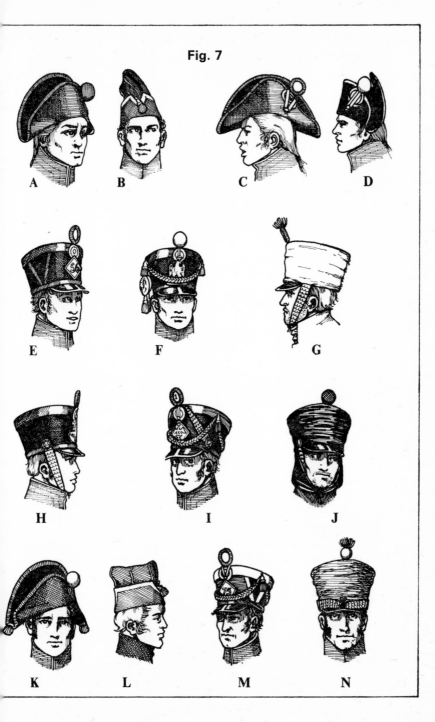

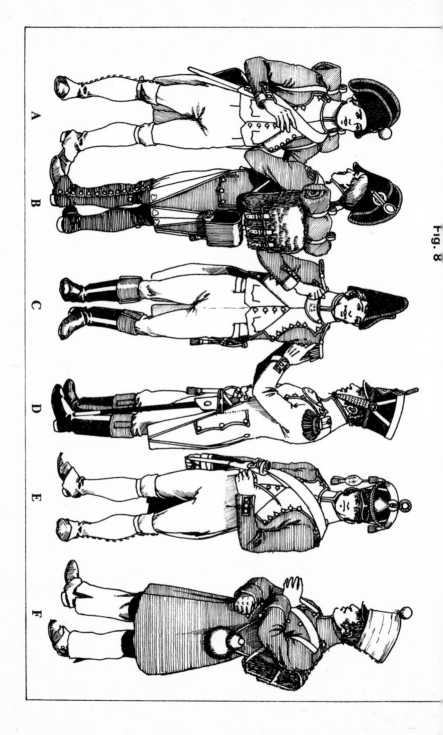

Fig. 8

was the gold lace upper band and chevrons. The cords and tassels, when worn, were also in gold lace.

(N) The 1810 shako, covered in light brown cloth and augmented by a white pom-pon with golden wool fringe. Under the cover, the shako is the same as for the men, but with the addition of a golden upper band.

Illustrated next are the costumes worn by fusiliers until the introduction of the 1810 model shako. The first five are largely parade dress figures (excepting figure D) and it should be born in mind that the rank and file would change from breeches to white trousers during campaign, and would remove the cords and tassels from their shakos. (Fig. 8).

1804–1806

(A) Here is a fusilier as he might have been on parade. His white gaiters specify that the season is summer.

(B) This figure is in marching order at about the time of the battle of Ulm. His greatcoat, rolled on the top of his pack, was paid for out of regimental funds, since they did not become official issue until April 25, 1806. Its colour depended largely upon the cloth that was locally available; grey or beige would seem most likely.

(C) An officer in service dress. His coat is identical to the men's but in finer cloth, with the addition of gold lace epaulettes. Note the yellow metal gorget plate hung under his collar; it was tied to the epaulette button on either side, and bore a white metal device — in this case a crowned Imperial eagle. On campaign he would sport white, grey or blue trousers (overalls) over the top of his boots. The sword knot was in gold lace.

1807

(D) Newly accoutred in white coat and 1807 shako this officer is in service dress. Note the regulation issue sword, it has brass fittings and golden knot. For parade dress he would simply add cords and tassels of gold.

1808–1810

(E) Returned to the usual blue coat, or perhaps never having received a white one in the first place, this man is in summer parade dress, designated by the addition of white cords and tassels and the white gaiters.

(F) In foul weather the fusilier would look much like this on campaign. His grey greatcoat has been unrolled from the pack and his shako has been covered by a waxed or oilskin cloth, tied at the back. Note the brown 'gourds' on his left hip. All infantry were required to carry a water bottle of some description, but there was never in the reported period a regulation issue.

Fig. 9 covers the last fusilier costumes under the empire.

1811–1812

(A) A fusilier during the Spanish Campaign. He has covered his shako with brown cloth. His white trousers having evidently worn out, he wears brown ones of local manufacture, tied about the ankles with strips of leather. Instead of the brown 'gourd' he carries a white metal canteen hung on a brown strap from his right shoulder. Note that he has covered his cartridge pouch with white cloth.

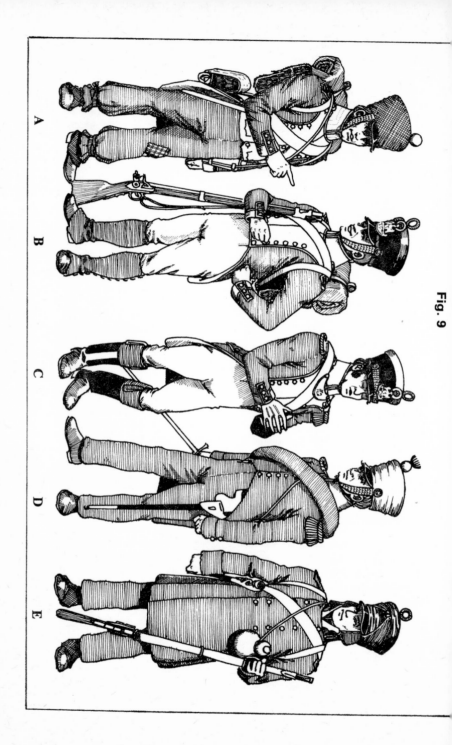

Fig. 9

(B) This is the regulation dress from 1813. Notice the new knee length gaiters.

(C) An officer in the regulation service dress. Though the tail of the coatee for the rank and file has been considerably reduced, the officers retained the previous length of tail, though it be narrower than before. The turnbacks are decorated with golden crowned 'N's.

(D) This officer on campaign wears a dark blue 'surtout' with red collar and copper buttons. His shako has a brown cover with a white pom-pon surmounted by a golden wool fringe. He has a dark blue greatcoat rolled over his shoulder and wears dark blue trousers. Note the regulation sword belt, and the red canteen strap.

(E) A fusilier in foul weather kit. His greatcoat is grey with pointed shoulder straps. It has the additional feature of red, three-pointed tabs on each side of the collar. His trousers are dark blue.

ELITE COMPANIES

A. The Voltigeurs:

In 1805 a new measure was inaugurated to utilise not only those men who were unsuited for precise drill and exercise, but also whose size was considered too small for their advancement into grenadier companies, and yet whose experience in warfare merited it. One company in every battalion was converted into a Voltigeur company.

Their rôle was to create a thin cover for the advancing ranks of fusilier companies and, in their deployed formation, pour fire into the enemy's massed lines. Return fire was almost useless in its effectiveness, for, unlike their opponents, the voltigeurs were widely spaced and hid behind whatever cover presented itself.

Light Cavalry was more often turned upon them and if they caught the voltigeurs dispersed on open ground, the devastation was complete. It was therefore pertinent not to let these lithe and elusive sharpshooters rush too far ahead of the bulk of the battalion, unless cover was nearby.

The innovation of these Light companies gave Napoleon a very distinct advantage over his opponents; for their addition meant a far more flexible infantry arm, the benefit of which over the old fashioned rigid infantry was apparent from the start. But it was not emulated by other armies until 1809.

The voltigeurs were clad in the standard infantry coat of the day, with the addition of epaulettes to distinguish their élite quality. The collars had yellow piping. The coat turnbacks were decorated with yellow bugle-horn patches. Further details of their dress and accoutrement can be seen in Fig. 10.

(A) Like the fusiliers, voltigeurs were equipped between 1804 and 1807 with a bicorn. The distinguishing feature was a large plume above the cockade, generally yellow over green.

(B) Upon the introduction of the 1806 model shako in 1807, a yellow pom-pon was added for voltigeurs, the plume could be added as well on special occasions. Cords and tassels were also adopted on these days and were usually green or yellow.

(C) The official voltigeurs' 1810 model shako was identical to that of the fusiliers, but with the addition of a short yellow plume. Very often

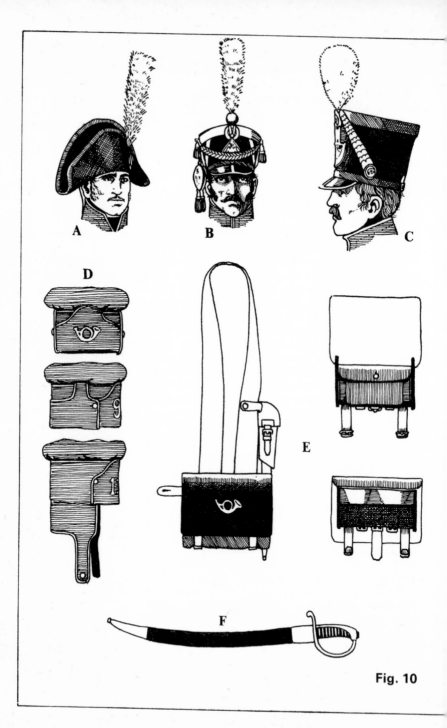

A   B   C

D

E

F

Fig. 10

though, we find that the upper and sometimes the lower bands were coloured yellow, chevrons of the same colour ornamenting the sides. The forbidden cords and tassels persisted in appearing, despite stringent orders to the contrary.

(D) The voltigeurs' fatigue cap after 1812. It was dark blue as for other companies with red, though sometimes yellow, piping and regimental number. Occasionally a yellow bugle-horn patch was sewn on instead of the number.

(E) The 1812 regulations specified that from 1813 voltigeurs were to discard the short sword they had carried previously, and adopt a combination cartridge-pouch and bayonet strap. The sword knots until the end of 1812 were usually yellow or green.

(F) The short sword itself, worn until 1813 on a strap on the left hip along with the bayonet.

Fig. 11 covers the changes of uniform from 1804 until 1810 with some typical figures as described below.

(A) Voltigeur of the 18th Line Infantry Regiment, full dress, 1805-1806. The plume on the bicorn hat is yellow over green. The dark blue coat has a yellow collar, piped in red, and white lapels and turnbacks all piped in red. The cuffs are red, piped in white, with dark blue cuff-slashes, piped in red. The epaulettes are green with yellow crescents. The red tassel of the fatigue cap can be seen hanging from beneath his cartridge-pouch.

(B) Officer of Voltigeurs in service dress, 1805-1806. The bicorn bears a yellow pom-pon. He wears the dark blue 'surtout' instead of the more expensive regulation habit, a common practise for officers in service dress. The 'surtout' has a yellow collar and golden epaulettes. He carries a standard epee, although élite company officers were permitted to carry a sabre, the sword knot is gold lace.

(C) Voltigeur of the 18th Line Infantry Regiment in service dress, 1807. The shako is unadorned except for a yellow pom-pon with a yellow woollen fringe. His coat is the new white issue. The collar is red, piped green, the lapels and turnbacks red, piped in red, the cuffs red, piped in white, the cuff-slashes white with red piping. The epaulettes are yellow with green crescents.

(D) Voltigeur of the 33rd Line Infantry Regiment in summer full dress, 1807. The shako has a yellow pom-pon and plume. The upper band is yellow as are the cords and tassels hanging from it. The coat is white with violet collar, lapels, turnbacks cuffs and cuff-slashes all piped in white. The epaulettes are yellow, also the turnback patches. The fatigue cap tassel and swordknot are yellow.

(E) Voltigeur of the 34th Line Infantry Regiment in foul weather kit 1808-1810. His shako is covered with black oilskin fabric, and has a yellow pom-pon. The overcoat is beige, the red epaulettes of which have yellow crescents and fringe. Note that the cartridge-pouch has been covered with white cloth. His voluminous grey trousers have been tucked into short white gaiters. His shoes are brown.

(F) Sergeant-Major of Voltigeurs of the 65th Line Infantry Regiment in campaign dress, 1808-1810. The pom-pon is red over green. The cording on the shako is green with red tassels. The dark blue coat has a yellow, red piped collar, the lapels and turnbacks are white, piped in red. The thirty years service required is denoted by three golden stripes on his left

73

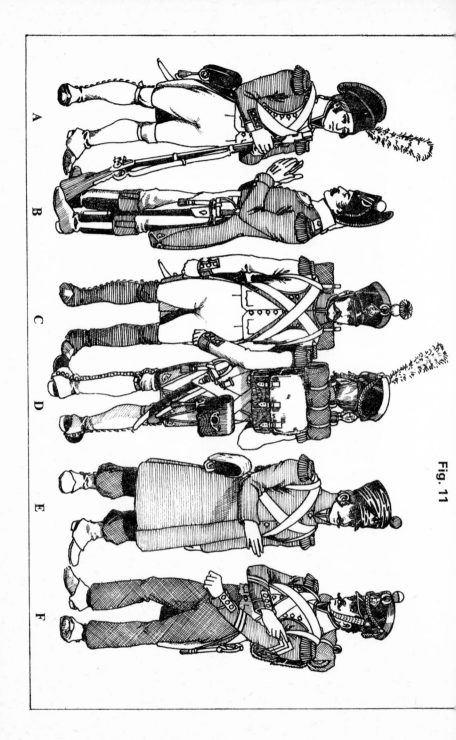

Fig. 11

74

Fig. 12

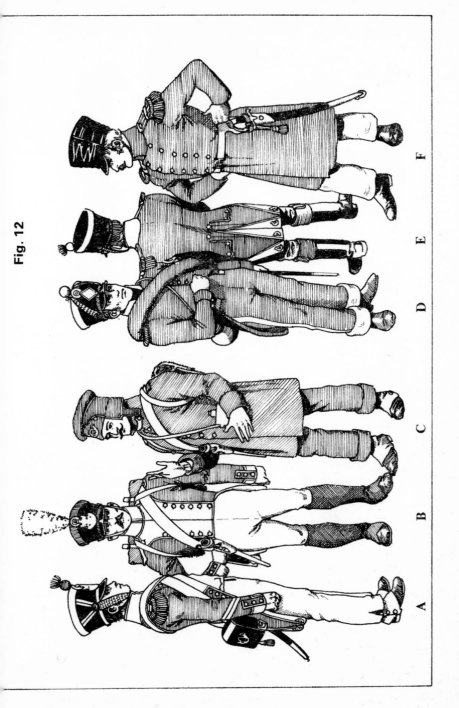

A   B   C   D   E   F

upper arm. His rank is further attested by two gold stripes, piped in red on both fore-arms. His trousers are brown, suggesting Peninsular service, and the gaiters white. The sword knot is green with a red fringe.

Fig. 12 concerns the dress of Voltigeurs from the time of issue of the 1810 model shako.

(A) Corporal of Voltigeurs in service dress, 1811-1812: the shako has been embellished with yellow upper and lower leather bands and yellow chevrons. The pom-pon is green with a yellow woollen fringe. The coat is dark blue with yellow collar, piped in blue, white lapels and turnbacks, piped in red, red cuffs, piped in white, and dark blue cuff-slashes piped in red. The epaulettes are green with yellow crescents. His rank is indicated by two orange stripes upon each forearm. The gaiters are white.

(B) Voltigeur in the 1812 regulation kit, 1813-1815: a plain shako, topped by a short yellow plume. The dark blue coat has yellow shoulder straps and collar, piped in blue. The cuffs are red, piped in white, the cuff-slashes dark blue, piped in red, the lapels and turnbacks are white; only the lapels are piped in red.

(C) Voltigeur in campaign dress, 1813-1815: the 'Pokalem' fatigue cap is dark blue with yellow piping and bugle-horn patch. The coat is grey with a yellow collar fastener. He has a white metal canteen hung by a white strap over his right shoulder. The trousers are a dark blue and he wears brown gaiters.

(D) Officer of Voltigeurs of the 18th Line Infantry Regiment, in campaign dress, 1813-1815: the shako has a golden upper band and a yellow pom-pon. The surtout is dark blue excepting the yellow collar and the epaulettes are golden. His dark blue overcoat is rolled over his left shoulder and a brown gourde is hung about the other. The trousers are dark blue with a white lining and have a broad yellow stripe on both outer seams.

(E) Officer of Voltigeurs in the 1812 regulation issue, 1813-1815: the shako has a golden upper band. The dark blue Spencer coat has a yellow collar, piped in red, white turnbacks, piped in red, and gold braid bugle-horn patches. The epaulettes are gold lace.

(F) Officer of Voltigeurs in campaign dress, 1813-1815: the shako is covered in black oilskin, fastened by cloth covered buttons on the side. The overcoat is dark blue with gold lace epaulettes. Officers would transfer the sword-belt to the outside of the coat; in this case it holds a sabre with a golden sword knot. His trousers are white.

B. The Grenadiers:

These were the original élites of Napoleon's infantry. Called from the ranks of fusiliers for their courage and experience on the field of battle, these men formed one company in every battalion.

Their position on the field was generally to the right of the fusiliers. When advancing, this position was usually maintained unless enemy fire was particularly heavy. In this event, they would be placed either at the front of the column to drag along the fusiliers with their steady pace, or at the back of the column to push the fusiliers forward. This latter position has a good deal to be said for it, since it provided the column with a strong untouched reserve with which to deliver the final blow, also a steady wall behind which repulsed fusiliers or voltigeurs might rally.

The grenadiers wore the standard infantry coat with the sole distinction

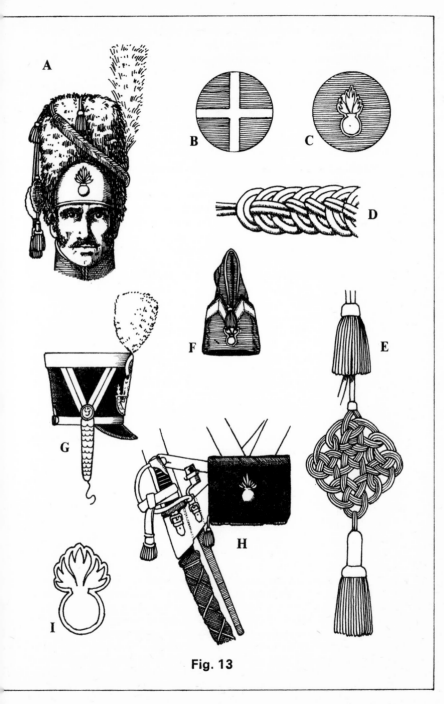

Fig. 13

of red epaulettes. In the early years until 1807, Grenadier companies would wear either the ordinary bicorn, topped by a tall red plume, or the more distinctive 'bonnet a poil'. Let us turn to the first set of grenadier drawings for details of this head-dress, Fig. 13.

(A) The 'bonnet a poil'. It was covered in black fur and had a copper plate at the front, upon which was embossed a flaming grenade device. The cords and tassels were red or white and passed on the left hand side beneath a cockade. Above this cockade was a long red plume. At the top of the back was a red patch upon which was stitched at first a white cross (B) and later a grenade patch, white upon an orange background, (C). This bearskin cap was reserved for parades and the battleground. On the march a bicorn would be worn and the bearskin was wrapped in protective cloth and tied to the back of the haversack.

(D) A detail of the cording for bearskins and shakoes.

(E) The tassels and a 'raquette' in detail. Bearskins and shakoes had a pair of these per unit.

(F) The fatigue cap until the introduction of the 'Pokalem' model in 1813. It is dark blue with red lace and piping. A grenade patch has been affixed to the front.

(G) The official 1812 pattern grenadier shako. The short plume is red as are the bands and chevrons.

(H) The small arms and cartridge pouch of the grenadiers until 1813. Thereafter they were supposed to adopt the combination cartridge-pouch and bayonet strap, as for voltigeurs and fusiliers, but they retained their short swords for some time after 1813. Notice the plume is wrapped in cloth about the short sword sheath. The sword knot is red and the cartridge-pouch bears a copper grenade device.

(I) The grenade patch in detail.

The next set of drawings (Fig. 14) show the uniform worn until 1811.

(A) Grenadier in full dress, 1804-1806: the bearskin has a red plume, white cords and tassels. The dark blue coat has red collar and cuffs, piped in white. The cuff slash in dark blue with red piping. The lapels and turnbacks are white, piped in red. The gaiters are white.

(B) Grenadier in winter full dress, 1804-1806: the uniform is identical to the previous one, except for the two red stripes on the left upper arm, denoting 20 years' service.

(C) Officer of Grenadiers in service dress, 1804-1806: the bearskin is identical to that of the rank and file, except that it bears golden cords and tassels. The coat is also the same, though made from better fabric, and has golden epaulettes. The gorget is polished yellow metal with a silver coloured device.

(D) Officer of Grenadiers of the 33rd Line Infantry Regiment, full dress 1807: the shako has golden upper band, chevrons, cords and tassels. The pom-pon is red with a red plume above it. The coat has violet collar, cuffs, cuff-slashes, lapels and turnbacks, all piped in white. The epaulettes and gorget are gold laced. The sword knot of the sabre is of gold lace. All buttons are copper.

(E) Grenadier in foul weather clothing, 1804-1806: an alternative to packing away the bearskin was to cover it like the shako in some waterproof cloth. The plume would be tied to the short sword sheath. The greatcoat is grey with no distinctions other than red epaulettes.

Fig. 14

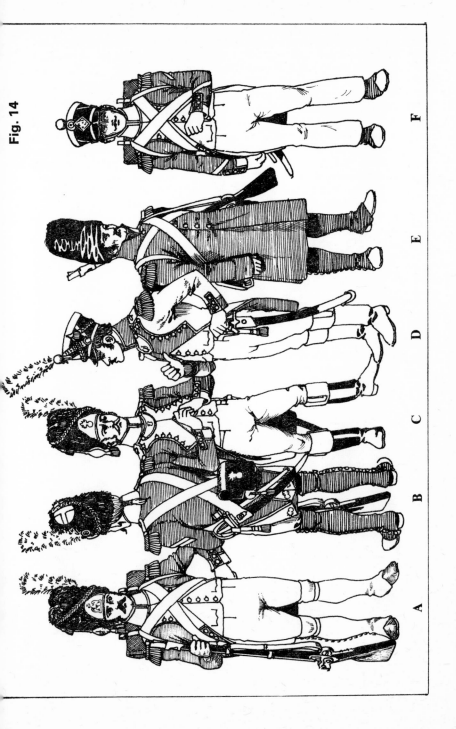

A   B   C   D   E   F

Fig. 15

(F) Sergeant of Grenadiers in service dress, 1808-1810: his 1806 model shako has a red upper band and pom-pon. His rank is indicated by a single yellow stripe on each forearm. The coat is identical, otherwise, to that shown at A in Fig. 14.

Fig. 15 depicts two officers in campaign dress.

(Left) Sous-Lieutenant of Grenadiers, 1804-1806: the bearskin is of particular interest, for instead of the more usual plate, it bears solely a grenade device, similar to those on the cartridge-pouches of the rank and file. He wears the familiar all dark blue surtout, decorated with golden epaulettes. His particular rank is indicated by two narrow strips of red piping down the body of each epaulette. He does not carry the conventional sabre or épée, but, curiously, a light cavalry sabre. The sheath is of white metal with brass fittings. The knot is golden and the belt red with golden lace edging. His fanciful boots have a black tassel at the front.

(Right) Sous-Lieutenant of Grenadiers in foul weather kit: the standard bearskin, minus the plume and cording. Note that for officers the cross on the red patch at the back is gold lace. His greatcoat is entirely dark blue with epaulettes identical to the other man. Buttons are copper. The sabre has the distinction of being hung from a black leather belt, edged in gold lace.

Like the men, officers would wear a bicorn for everyday dress. Apart from the greatcoat they were also permitted to don a long dark blue cape in inclement weather. This garment was fastened usually at the neck by a gilt chain.

The last plate in this section on élite companies concerns the dress of Grenadiers from 1811 to 1815, as shown in Fig. 16.

(A) Grenadier in campaign dress, 1811-1813: his oilskin covered shako has a red pom-pon. The greatcoat, looking to be of foreign origin, is brown with red epaulettes and collar fastening. The cartridge pouch is foreign, though a regular grenade device has been added. A brown gourde is hung over the other shoulder, and he seems to have misplaced his short sword. The baggy grey trousers have been tucked into short white gaiters.

(B) Officer of Grenadiers in campaign dress, 1813-1815: his shako has a brown cloth cover and a red pom-pon and fringe. The surtout is dark blue with red piping around the collar, the cuffs, down the front and along the turnbacks. His gorget is gilt. A white metal canteen hangs on a white strap and his rolled, dark blue, greatcoat is tied to his back by a brown leather strap. The breeches are white, the sword knot golden.

(C) Officer of Grenadiers in 1812 regulation kit, 1813-1815: his shako has a golden upper band, red pom-pon and fringe. The dark blue Spencer coat has red collar and cuffs, piped in white, dark blue cuff-slashes, piped in red, white lapels and turnbacks, piped in red. The gorget and epaulettes are gilt, as is the sword knot.

(D) Grenadier in 1812 regulation kit, 1813-1815: the shako has red upper, lower bands and chevrons. The short plume is red. His coatee is identical to the officer's excepting for the length of the skirt and the red epaulettes. Note that he has, contrary to edict, retained his short sword, the sword knot of which is red.

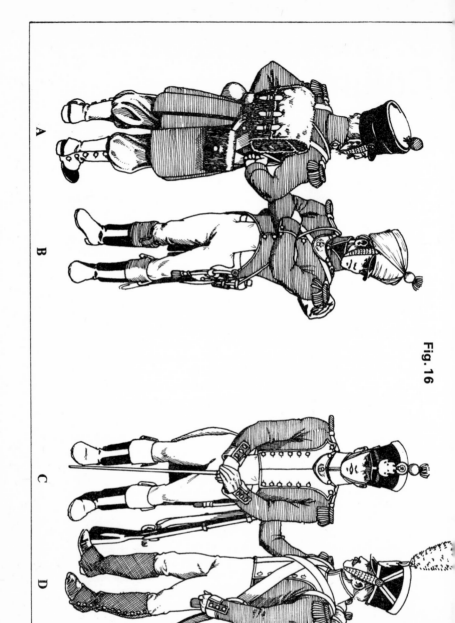

A B

Fig. 16

C D

5: The Heads of Column

IN this section we examine the 'heads of column' of Napoleon's infantry. This term includes sappers, standard-bearers and high-ranking officers. The drum-majors and musicians who also come into this category will be covered in the next section since the subject is more extensive.

1. Standard Bearers:

In the Musée de Versailles hangs a painting that encompasses in its subject all the fervour, pride and devotion that Napoleonic troops felt towards their colours; it is the 'Distribution des Aigles' by David.

On this emotional date of December 5th 1804, we see high-ranking officers falling over one another to hold their Eagles just that fraction closer to the Emperor; those at the back struggling to raise theirs that inch or two higher than their fellows' that it might catch the Emperor's eye. The flag itself was unimportant next to the bronze eagle that perched at the top of the pole. Its mighty wings half spread, its imperious head turned to one side, its powerful claws clutching a solid bronze wedge, it represented the promise of the Revolution, to be fulfilled in the destiny of France under the Emperor Napoleon. For Napoleon represented the end of interior strife and the beginning of a new era in which the enlightened Republic would spread the influence of the people to the oppressed populations of Europe. It was physical might, with spiritual strength, and was immovable from its lofty perch.

It is important to remember the strong spiritual determination that drove the troops onwards in these early days; the War Department certainly did, for the 1804 standards were issued to every battalion of the infantry, and the standard was carried by a Sergeant-Major specially selected by the regimental Colonel for his resilience in battle.

Fig. 17 depicts its position when the battalion was deployed in line. The standard would bear not only the battalion number, but also the regimental name and number.

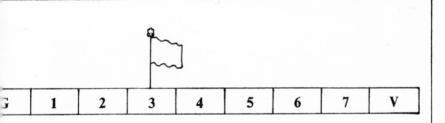

Fig. 17

On February 18 1808, an Imperial Decree specified that the number of standards was to be reduced to one per regiment; battalions retained their standards until they were captured or lost. The regimental standard was to be carried by an ensign of no less than ten years service, having been present at Ulm, Austerlitz; Jena and Friedland. With this man selected, a bodyguard was created.

This bodyguard comprised of a 2nd and 3rd Colour-Bearer; both veteran, senior NCOs they marched on both sides of the ensign bearing a pike, each bearing a distinctive banner: that of the 2nd bearer, red, and that of the 3rd white. They were further armed with a brace of pistols apiece, carried in a double holster hung upon their chest. A colour party with this bodyguard is illustrated on the cover.

Behind these three would march, in two rows, four sappers and a sapper-corporal. But despite these safeguards many standards were captured or lost during the course of the campaigns. Below is a list of those lost at the various battles.

The 1805 campaign:
Caldiero: That of the 1st battalion of the 5th Line Regt.
Austerlitz: That of the 1st battalion of the 4th Line Regt.

The 1807 campaign:
Eylau: That of the 1st battlion of the 18th Line Regt.
      That of the 1st battalion of the 44th Line Regt.
      A standard of the 51st Line Regt.
Heilsberg: A standard of the 55th Line Regt.
Friedland: A standard of the 15th Line Regt.

The 1809 campaign:
Innsbruck: That of the 3rd battalion of the 2nd Line Regt.
Pardenone: That of the 1st battalion of the 35th Line Regt.
Wagram: That of the 3rd battalion of the 4th Line Regt.
      The standard of the 106th Line Regt.

The capitulation of Martinique:
3 Eagles of the 82nd Line Regt.
That of the 2nd battalion of the 26th Line Regt.

The capitulation of Guadeloupe:
The standard of the 66th Line Regt.

The 1812 campaign:
Krasnoe: That of the 35th Line Regt.
      That of the 18th Line Regt.
Berezina: That of the 44th Line Regt.
      That of the 126th Line Regt.

The Peninsular campaign:
Barossa: That of the 8th Line Regt.
Foz de Arunce: That of the 39th Line Regt.
Arapiles: That of the 22nd Line Regt.
      That of the 62nd Line Regt.
Capitulation of Madrid: That of the 51st Line Regt.
Capitulation of Pampelune: That of the 52nd Line Regt.
Capitulation of Lerida: That of the 42nd Line Regt.

The 1813 campaign:
Katzbach: That of the 134th Line Regt.
That of the 146th Line Regt.
That of the 148th Line Regt.
Kulm: That of the 21st Line Regt.
That of the 33rd Line Regt.
Leipzig: That of the 145th Line Regt.
That of the 140th Line Regt.
Neuss: That of the 150th Line Regt.

The 1814 campaign:
Wittenberg capitulation: That of the 123rd Line Regt.
Pithiviers: That of the 4th Line Regt.
Glogau: That of the 151st Line Regt.

The '100 days' campaign:
Waterloo: That of the 45th Line Regt.
That of the 105th Line Regt.
The standard pattern for the colours is shown in colour on page 29.

Fig. 18 shows the uniforms of the Standard-bearers from 1804 through 1815.

(A) Sergeant-Major Colour bearer of the 4th Line Infantry Regiment, winter full dress, 1804-1806. The bicorn hat has four orange slashes on each side (two on each side of the back) and orange tassels in the angles; these decorated the bicorns of the 4th until December 1807 to commemorate their gallantry at the battle of Arcola. The hat has a white pom-pon on the top. The dark blue coat has a red collar, cuffs and cuff-slashes, all piped in white. The lapels and turnbacks are white, piped in red. The shoulder straps are dark blue with red piping. His rank is indicated by the two gold, red piped, stripes on each fore-arm. The sword knot is red, piped in gold, with a red and gold tassel.

(B) Sergeant-Major Colour Bearer of the 3rd Line Infantry Regiment in Summer full dress, 1807: the bicorn is embellished with a red, carrot shaped pom-pon. The coat is white with green collar, lapels, cuffs and cuff-slashes, all piped in white. The turnbacks are white with green piping, numeral and star patches. The rank stripes have been changed to silver on a green background. The epaulettes are red with silver crescents and red and silver fringes.
The sword knot is silver lace, piped in red, with a red tassel knob and a silver and red tassel fringe. All buttons have been changed to white metal.

(C) Ensign Colour Bearer of Fusiliers, full dress 1808-1810: the upper band and chevrons of the shako are gold, as are the cords and tassels. The dark blue coat has red collar and cuffs, piped in white, dark blue cuff-slashes, piped in red, white lapels and turnbacks, piped in red. The epaulettes are gold lace and the sword-belt buckle is gilt. The colour strap, worn over the left shoulder is red with gold edging.

(D) Ensign of Fusiliers, Colour Bearer, of the 153rd Line Infantry Regiment, campaign dress, 1813-1815: the bicorn is plain excepting for the gold lace holding the cockade in place. The coat is beige with gold lace epaulettes. The belt buckle and sword knot are gold lace. The colour holder is red with a gold lace fringe.

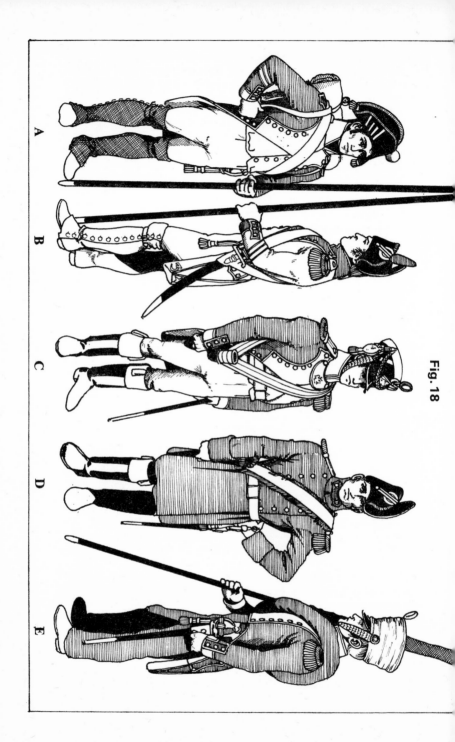

Fig. 18

(E) Ensign of Fusiliers, Colour Bearer, of the 45th Line Infantry Regiment, 1815: the shako is covered in brown cloth and bears a white disc pom-pon. He wears the standard Spencer coatee with red collar and cuffs, piped in white, dark blue cuff-slashes, piped in red, white lapels and turnbacks, piped in red, and golden epaulettes. His greatcoat is dark blue and is rolled over his left shoulder. The trousers are also dark blue. The sword knot is red piped in gold with a red and gold tassel.

Battalions at first carried the entire standard into battle, but were later prohibited from doing so, carrying only the pole with Eagle atop. Nonetheless, we can safely assume that a good many regiments did so anyway. For the march, the banner would be wrapped about the staff and covered in protective cloth.

2. The officers:

We have already seen company officers, it only remains to clear up a few points and describe the dress of senior officers. Up to the rank of Colonel, the order of seniority was as follows, from the bottom up:

> Adjutant-sous-Officier.
> Sous-Lieutenant.
> Lieutenant.
> Capitaine.
> Chef-de-Bataillon.
> Major.
> Colonel.

From the beginning of the Napoleonic period, officers were dressed in essentially identical uniforms to the men, the sole difference being the superior quality of the cloth, buttons and buckles.

The turnbacks of the habit were decorated with golden grenades for Grenadiers, golden bugle-horns for Voltigeurs and golden crowned 'N's for Fusiliers, also numbers, eagles or stars. Above company level, senior officers would generally bear golden grenades on the turnbacks.

All grades of officers would frequently exchange the habit for the more comfortable 'surtout'. This had a single row of buttons, usually nine in number, that fastened the dark blue 'surtout' to the waist. Most often this coat was totally blue, excepting for Voltigeur officers for whom a yellow collar was reserved. However, many had red collars, cuffs and piping; also red cuffs piped in white and red collars piped in blue. Just about any combination of the above was possible, excepting of course, the yellow collar. The turnbacks would have the same ornaments as the habit.

With the introduction of the white coat in 1807, the surtout remained blue, though officers were required to change their blue habits for the new white ones. Many officers acquired themselves new white coats with the distinctive facings, despite the fact that the rest of the regiment did not.

The rank of the wearer was indicated by the epaulettes. Fig. 19 depicts the differences.

(A) Epaulettes of an Adjutant-sous-Officier: the fringed epaulette was worn on the left shoulder and the unfringed one on the right. The body of the epaulette is red with two stripes of gold traversing its length. The crescent is gold and the fringe is composed of two layers of gold and three layers of red silk.

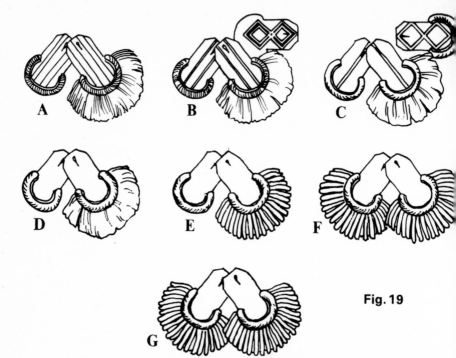

Fig. 19

(B) Epaulettes of a Sous-Lieutenant: note the same positioning of the epaulettes. These were gold bodied with two rows of scarlet silk piping, either along the length of the body or, most frequently, towards the end of the Empire, forming a squared loop. Gold crescents and fringe.

(C) Epaulettes of a Lieutenant: the same arrangement of the epaulettes. They had a gold body with a single strip of scarlet piping and gold crescents and fringe.

(D) Epaulettes of Capitaine: the fringed epaulette on the left and the plain one on the other. Both are gold.

(E) Epaulettes of a Chef-de-Bataillon: a heavy bullion fringed epaulette on the left and an unfringed one on the right.

(F) The epaulettes of a Major.

(G) The epaulettes of a Colonel.

A Colonel 'en second' and a Major 'en second' served with each regiment, they bore the same epaulettes as the Colonel and Major respectively, but with the difference of a single strip of ponceau piping travelling down the body.

The Adjutant-sous-Officier, an officer of General Staff, wore identical uniform to the lieutenants with the exceptions of not wearing a gorget or a sword knot.

The Adjutant-Major was a general staff officer as well, and wore the epaulettes of whatever his rank, but in the reverse position.

The bicorn hat was standard issue in the early years, and bore a white pom-pon for senior officers, green or yellow for Voltigeur officers, red for Grenadier officers and of company colour for Fusiliers. It was often topped by a plume of like colour for grand occasions. The pom-pons were of no fixed shape or size. The bicorns were sometimes further embellished by tassels in the corners, the weight of which depended on the rank of the wearer.

With the introduction of the shako in 1807, the officer's version bore a gold braid upper band and frequently golden chevrons. Golden cords and tassels were added as occasion demanded, as well as the plume to the pom-pon.

With the 1810 model shako, a more specific ornamentation was derived by 1813:

Colonels : An upper band of gold lace, 35mm in width, followed by a second 15mm in width below that. A golden round or tulip shaped pom-pon supporting a white plume.

Majors : An upper band, also 35mm thick, of gold, followed by a silver one 15mm in width. The plume again with a golden pom-pon, was red over white.

Chef-de-Bataillon : An upper gold band 35mm wide and an all red plume.

Capitaines : A gold band 30mm wide and a gold tufted company coloured pom-pon.

Lieutenants :An upper band 25mm in width and either a fringed pom-pon, red for Grenadiers, green or yellow for Voltigeurs, or a plain one of company colour, sometimes also bearing a fringe, but of gold.

Sous-Lieutenants: An upper band of gold, 20mm in width, but with the same pom-pon arrangement as the lieutenants.

Adjutant-Majors : A large white carrot-shaped pom-pon.

Adjutant-sous-Officiers : A white pom-pon and a gold band.

The shako band of the Adjutant-Major would, of course, depend on his rank. The headgear of the Colonels and Majors 'en second' would be identical to the acting ones. Gold cords and tassels were retained for full dress.

The bicorn was retained throughout the period for off duty and society dress. This last, consisted of either the habit or the surtout coat, off-white breeches, cotton stockings, and black shoes with silver buckles. In winter, the white breeches would be replaced by blue or black pairs and the white stockings by blue or black woollen ones. The fatigue cap was also worn, made of finer material and laced and piped in gold instead of red.

On campaign, the breeches would often as not be replaced by trousers of blue, white, or grey cloth, worn on the outside of the boot and with leather reinforced inside legs for mounted officers.

Fig. 20 illustrates the sidearms and gorget device of the officers.

(A and D) These are typical épees as carried by all Fusilier officers; some élite company and high ranking officers would also carry them.

(B and C) The sabres carried by élite company officers and senior officers. The blades were between 2ft 3½ins. and 2ft 6½ins. long.

Senior, mounted officers would also wear cavalry sabres on occasion.

(E) The type of sword belt used for épées and sabres, the sabre model differed solely by the amount of space made for the sheath.

(F, G and H) These are all silver devices mounted on the jugulars, or

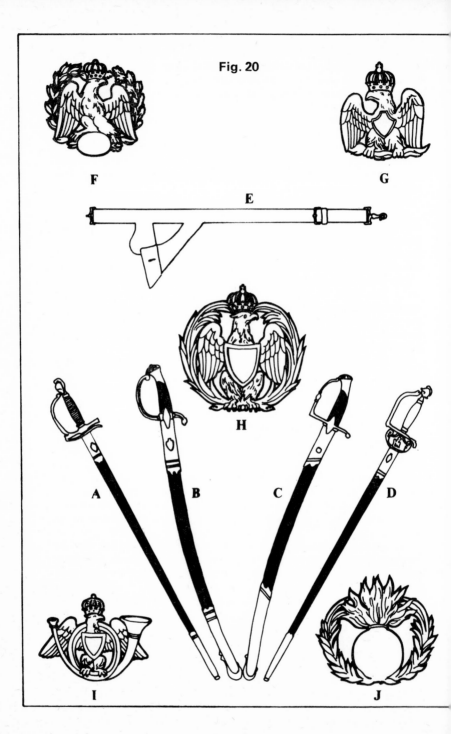

Fig. 20

gorgets, of Fusilier and senior officers. The gorgets were golden and were attached by a silver thread from silver buttons to the bottoms of the epaulettes. The shields bore the regimental number.

(I and J) The devices for the élite companies. That of Grenadiers, on the right, could also be a plain grenade or have the regimental number inscribed upon its shell.

Mounted officers would have a dark blue saddle cover edged in gold lace, with matching twin pistol holsters. Until 1813, the regimental number or a grenade appeared in the angles of the cloth, stitched in gold thread. Thereafter the saddle-cloths became plain, excepting the gold lacing which was of 50mm in width. Colonels and Majors added a second strip, 15mm wide, to this.

Fig. 21 shows some typical senior officers.

(A) Colonel of the 18th Line Regiment, full dress, 1804-1806: the bicorn has golden lace and slashes. In each corner are golden tassels. The plume is red over white over blue. The dark blue coat has a red collar, piped in white, white lapels and white turnbacks, piped in red. The twin epaulettes are golden as are the gorget and sword knot.

(B) Major (Lieutenant-Colonel) of the 26th Line Regiment in society dress, 1808-1810: the bicorn is quite plain excepting for a white, ellipse shaped pom-pon and golden tassels at the corners. The dark blue coat has red collar and cuffs, piped in white, white lapels, cuff-slashes and turnbacks, piped in red. The epaulettes have silver bodies. The belt buckle is yellow with a silver device.

(C) Colonel in full dress and overcoat, 1811-1813: the shako has a white plume upon a golden pom-pon. The upper band, cords, and tassels are also gold. The coat is totally dark blue with gilt buttons. The epaulettes are gold lace.

(D) Major in undress: the dark blue fatigue cap has golden lace, piping and tassel. The dark blue surtout has a red collar and silver bodied gold epaulettes.

3. The Sappers:

The 'sapeurs', 'soldats charpentiers' or 'pioneers' were an integral part of the head of infantry columns. Their duty lay in clearing the path for the following troops, destroying with their large axes impediments such as hedges, fences, gates or doorways that could slow the advance of the column.

The organisational decree to the army of February 18, 1808 was the Empire's first acknowledgement of their position. There were to be four in every battalion, part of the grenadier company, under the command of a sapper corporal.

Previously their numbers were most irregular, as these figures, recorded in 1804, portray:

The 3rd Line Regt: 16 sappers.	The 25th Line Regt: 19 sappers.
The 10th Line Regt: 12 sappers.	The 43rd Line Regt: 8 sappers.
The 14th Line Regt: 19 sappers.	The 46th Line Regt: 13 sappers.
The 19th Line Regt: 9 sappers.	The 64th Line Regt: 12 sappers.
The 22nd Line Regt: 9 sappers.	The 87th Line Regt: 13 sappers.

Sappers were armed with a large axe and a short sword or sabre. The sabres could be straight, curved, or saw-toothed, with a plain, cock's or eagle's headed hilt. These weapons were augmented by a carbine and

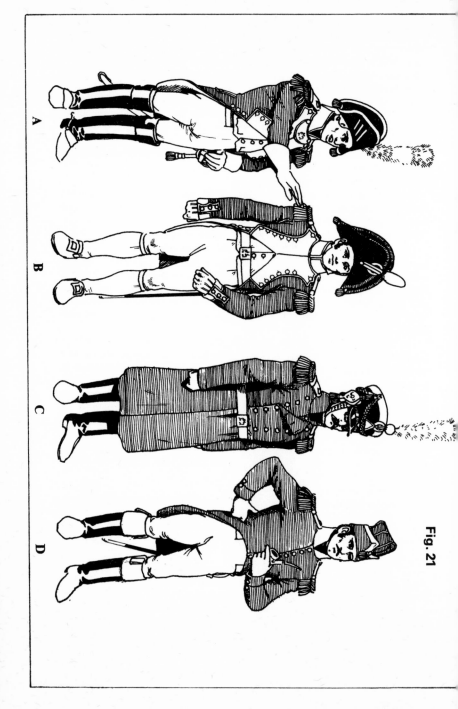

Fig. 21

bayonet, and occasionally a brace of pistols as well. Ammunition was kept in a cartridge pouch on the right hip if the axe holder was not used. Where the axe holder was employed, a cartridge pouch attached to a waist belt was utilised, carrying a maximum of twenty cartridges.

Sappers were supposed to be dressed in the same manner as the grenadiers. The bearskin would not, however, bear a copper plate, and a pair of red crossed axe patches were added to the upper sleeves of the habit. Their rough function necessitated their wearing a pair of cuffed gloves and a large blancoed skin apron.

As the musicians' uniforms were embellished, so were those of the sappers, and we see many with gaudy colour changes effectuated on the facings. Some even had the habit cloth changed from dark blue to such colours as crimson and sky blue.

Sappers were required to exchange their bearskins for shakos after 1807 but documentary evidence suggests they clung to them with even more tenacity than the grenadiers.

Fig. 22 shows examples of Sappers and their equipment.

(A) Sapper of the 18th Line Regiment, 1804-1806. This is a fairly representative figure of the early dress of the 'sapeurs'. The bearskin has a red plume and white cords and tassels. The dark blue coat is standard, with red collar, piped in white, white lapels and turnbacks, piped in red, and red epaulettes. Note that the red axe patch has been augmented with a red grenade patch. The belt has a copper, grenade embossed buckle.

(B) Sapper Corporal of the 33rd Line Regiment, 1807. His bearskin is identical to that of A. The white coat has violet collar, lapels and turnbacks, all piped in white. The red epaulettes have the distinction of yellow crescents. The sleeve patches are of the facing colour, violet, and have been sewn over two red service stripes on the left arm. The rank stripes on the fore-arms are orange. The cross-belts have been decorated with copper scaled buckles and grenade devices. Note that a pair of pistols complete his heavy armament.

(C) Another popular form of headdress was this 'colpack' form of bearskin. The bag hanging down the left hand side is red with white piping, the pom-pon and plume are red.

(D) The crossed axe patch.

(E) An alternative form of epaulette seen on some habits. It has been scaled in copper to protect the shoulders. The crescent and fringe remain red.

(F) One of the many types of axe used during the course of the Empire. No regulation model existed.

(G) One of the many forms of sabre carried by sappers. The lighter short sword was understandably more popular for campaigns.

(H) The Year IX model carbine or 'mousqueton'.

(I) Another popular model, this one dates back to 1786.

(J) The standard axe holder, worn on the right hip. Note the diminuative cartridge pouch with a crossed axe device, it carried only six cartridges and was often used in conjunction with a larger one attached to a waistbelt.

After 1812, sappers were issued with the Spencer coatee. This was embellished with the usual axe patch. Their equipment remained essentially the same.

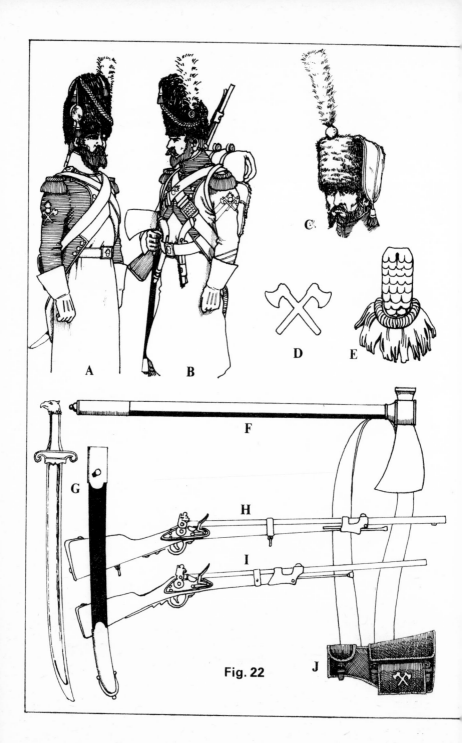

Fig. 22

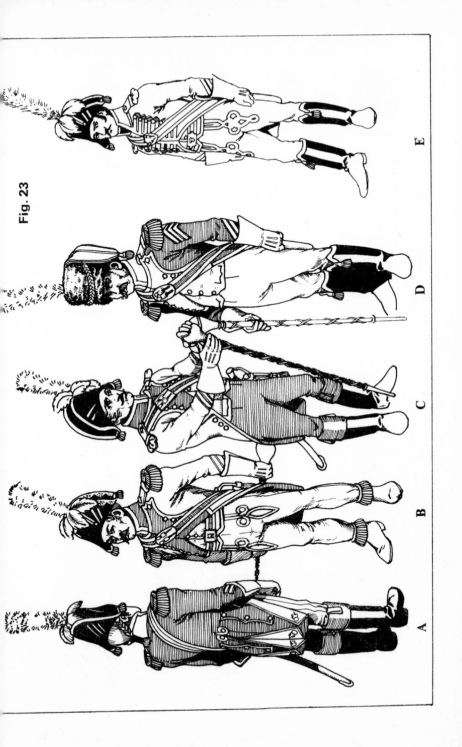

Fig. 23

6: The Musicians

IN their cantonments, on the battlefield and upon the capture of enemy towns, the infantry regiments of Napoleon paraded. At their head marched the musicians and it was these that most impressed the crowds; inspiring by their fine martial bearing, young men of all classes to the standard, to share in the glory of Imperial conquests.

Each regiment was officially permitted eight musicians, but many colonels went to considerable expense engaging above and beyond this number, of civilian bandsmen to swell the colourful head of column. Bassoons, clarinets, trombones, oboes, trumpets, bass drums, snare drums, cymbals, and other instruments were used. But parades and triumphant marches were not the bandsmen's sole function, for in Napoleonic times the music played a vital role on the battlefield as well.

Fifteen paces behind the first battalion marched a double row of drummers, pacing the advance, and behind these the musicians blared out a martial air, to uphold and compel the courage of the men. Once the infantry were engaged, the band would lay down its instruments and risk their lives distributing ammunition, or carrying the badly wounded to the comparative safety of the field hospitals. But these were only the bandsmen. The drummers' rôle (no pun intended) continued, for with no other form of communication orders had to be conveyed to the ranks by their skill alone, relaying the verbal messages of the superior officers with special drum signals, or carrying messages by hand. These drummers were led by a drum-major, the subject of the first part of this chapter.

1. Drum-Majors.

Drum-Majors held the rank of sergeant-major and bore therefore, two golden stripes, embellished with scarlet piping, upon each sleeve.

The coat itself was dependent on whatever particular fantasy struck the Colonel and what his wallet could stand. Despite repeated circulars, reminding the colonels that the coat should be but distinctive of the rank of the wearer, they continued to indulge in changing the facing colours, adding gold lace wherever space permitted, and festooning the headgear with all manner of colourful plumes. Since all other musicians wore similar coloured uniforms to the drum-major, we can imagine the spectacle the head of column presented, and the consequent rivalry between colonels to have the largest, most smartly dressed group of musicians in the infantry.

Fig. 23 shows their costumes in but some diversity.

(A) Drum-major of the 18th Line Regiment, 1804-1806. The bicorn has been laced and ornamented in gold. The plume is red over white over blue. Three ostrich plumes, red, white and blue respectively, further augment the headgear. His jacket is dark blue with a red collar, edged in gold lace, and white turnbacks, piped in red, bearing gold grenade devices. The pockets are simulated by red piping and the two buttons at the top of the skirt vent are ornamented with gold lace, the gloves

Fig. 24

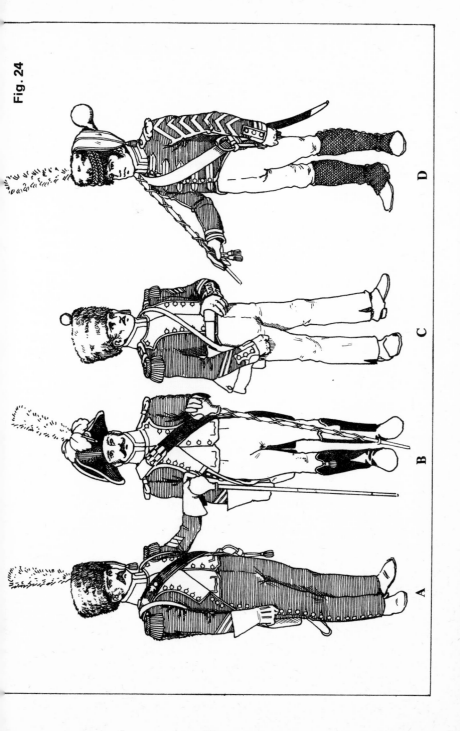

A   B   C   D

being white, and also edged in gold. The breeches are off-white with a strip of gold lace down each outer seam.

(B) Drum-Major of the 33rd Line Regiment, 1807. The bicorn bears golden lace ornaments. The plume is white with three ostrich plumes about its base, one red and two turquoise. His white coat has a violet collar, lapels and turnbacks, all laced in gold. The epaulettes are golden and both belts are red with gold lace. The shortcoat and the trousers are white with golden lace, as are the gloves. His ankle-boots have a golden fringe.

(C) Drum-Major of the 26th Line Regiment, 1808-1810. The bicorn has gold lace ornaments, a white plume, about which are clustered two red ostrich plumes and one dark blue one. The coat is red with dark blue collar, lapels and turnbacks, all laced in gold. He has adopted golden trefoils instead of the fringed epaulettes. The sword belt is dark blue, edged in gold, and the breeches are dark blue.

(D) Drum-Major of the 65th Line Regiment, 1808-1810. He wears a black fur 'colpack' cap. It has a white plume, golden cords and tassels, and a red, gold edged, bag hanging down the left side. His coat is dark blue with a red collar, white lapels and turnbacks, all laced in gold. The gold, red piped, stripes on his left upper arm denote thirty years' service. The sword knot is golden and the belt is red, laced in gold. The short coatee is red. His boots have golden edging and golden fringed red tassels.

(E) Drum-Major of the 5th Line Regiment, 1810. This curious costume is probably a throwback to the white cloth regulations of 1806, for silver edging is utilised throughout, instead of golden lace. The bicorn has silver decorations and white plume with three white ostrich plumes. The coat and breeches are sky blue, including the coat collar, and decorated entirely with silver lace. The two belts are crimson with silver edging. The boots are black with silver lacing and tassels.

Fig. 24 depicts the trend towards simplification in drum-major's dress as the Empire's resources became more fully stretched.

(A) Drum-Major of the 65th Line Regiment, 1810-1812. Gone now are the cords and tassels, the 'colpack' retains only the white plume and the red, gold edged, bag. The dark blue coat has a red collar, edged in gold, and white lapels and turnbacks, piped in red. The epaulettes are golden, as are the stripes, though these have red piping. The coatee is red with the addition of golden piping. The tight white breeches have been discarded in favour of dark blue overalls. These have a single row of copper buttons down each outside seam. The sword knot is golden.

(B) Drum-Major of the 4th Line Regiment, 1811, has a relatively plain bicorn, edged in golden lace, with a white plume about the base of which are two red and one blue ostrich plumes. The dark blue coat has a red collar and green lapels and turnbacks, all edged in gold lace. Golden trefoil epaulettes are being worn. His sword belt and gloves are, curiously, black. His boots have gold piping and tassels.

(C) Drum-Major of the 34th Line Regiment, 1813. A plain 'colpack' excepting for a red pom-pon and bag, piped in gold. The dark blue coat has a red collar, edged in gold, and white lapels and turnbacks, piped in red. The cuffs are red, edged in gold, and the tri-pointed cuff-slashes white, edged in gold. The epaulettes are red with golden edging and

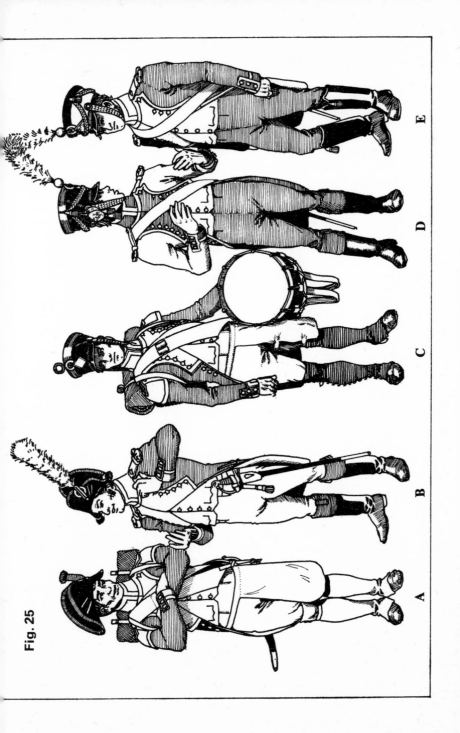

Fig. 25

crescents. The belt is white with a copper buckle. The provisions bag is also white, as are his trousers.

(D) Drum-Major of the 153rd Line Regiment, 1813-1815. The 'colpack' has a white plume, golden cords and tassels, and a red, gold piped, bag. He wears the new Imperial Livery, a dark green coat with intricate lace that is the subject of one of the colour plates, with a few notable differences. The red collar not only bears the essentially yellow livery lace, but also an interior strip of plain white lace. This same applies to the cuffs. The seven chevrons of lace on the sleeves are linked on the seams by strips of the same. The epaulettes are golden trefoils. He carries a light short sword of regulation issue, it has a golden knot.

Notice that the short sword or sabre belt carries a small copper plate. This held a pair of miniature drumsticks. A further distinction of the drum-major's rank and position was his copper ended baton. This had a cord about it, usually silver, that ended in two similarly coloured tassels.

2. Corporal-Tambours:

These men were corporals of grenadier drummers and were required to instruct the battalion's drummers. They wore the same uniform as the grenadier drummers, with the addition of their two rank stripes on each sleeve. A further distinction was their carrying a slightly smaller version of a drum-major's staff or baton. A Corporal-Tambour is shown in colour on page 25.

Let us now turn our attention to the drummers themselves. Each infantry company was permitted two and they were dressed in a usually similar uniform to the drum-major. Their equipment consisted of a short sword, worn over the right shoulder, and a drum-strap with two drum-stick holders. The drum itself was made of copper and had blue hoops, though some companies insisted on tri-colour stripes upon them. White cords held the ends together, and two straps attached to the case permitted the drum to be borne on the back. When slung on the shoulder-strap for playing, it would ride on the left thigh, most drummers therefore acquired an apron to protect the trousers and leg. They became regulation issue in 1811.

Fig. 25 depicts the uniforms of fusilier company drummers and also a few bandsmen.

3. Bandsmen, Drummers and Cornets:

(A) Drummer of Fusiliers of the 18th Line Regiment, 1804-1806. He wears a black bicorn that bears a light blue cylindrical pom-pon with a red fringe. The bicorn has two red slashes on either side. His dark blue coat has a red collar, laced in yellow, and light blue lapels, shoulder-wings and cuffs, all laced in yellow. The cuff-slashes and shoulder-straps are dark blue and piped in red. The turnbacks remain white and are piped in red.

(B) Bandsman of the 18th Line Regiment, 1804-1806. His bicorn has a white plume and has yellow slashes and tassels. His coat is identical to that of the drummer above, excepting for the addition of yellow trefoil epaulettes. The sword knot is yellow.

(C) A Drummer of Fusiliers, 1808-1810. The 1806 model shako has no particular distinction from that of the men. The dark blue coat has red collar, cuffs and shoulder-wings, all edged in yellow lace. The lapels are white with both red piping and yellow lace. The turnbacks have but the red piping, as do the dark blue shoulder-straps and cuff-slashes.

(D) Bandsman of the 26th Line Regiment, 1808-1810. The shako has been embellished with white cords and tassels, and a white pom-pon and plume, this last with a dark blue tip. His red coat matches that of the drum-major and has dark blue collar, lapels, cuffs, cuff-slashes and turnbacks, all laced in yellow. The trefoil epaulettes are yellow. The coatee is white and the trousers dark blue.

(E) Bandsman of the 65th Line Regiment, 1808-1810. He wears an extraordinary yellow shako with black leather bands. The plume and all the cords and tassels are white. The coat is dark blue with red collar, lapels and cuff-slashes, all laced in yellow. The cuff itself is dark blue with yellow lacing, the turnbacks white with red piping and yellow lace. He wears yellow trefoils. He has acquired a pair of brown breeches and wears them beneath yellow piped and tasseled boots.

In grenadier companies the drummers would follow the drum-major's precedent, but with the addition of bearskin caps or shakoes, depending on which the grenadiers bore. The grenadiers often replaced one of the two drummers with a fifer, who, unlike the drummers, carried a musket and also a cartridge-pouch on a cross-strap.

Fig. 26 shows some drummers and musicians in typical dress.

(A) Drummer of Grenadiers of the 57th Line Regiment 1804-1806. The bicorn has a red carrot shaped pom-pon and red slashes on each side. He wears the white fatigue coatee, it has red collar, cuffs and epaulettes (these having been transferred from the shoulders of the dark blue habit). The trousers are white.

(B) Fifer of Grenadiers of the 18th Line Regiment, 1804-1806. His bearskin has a red plume and white cords and tassels. The dark blue coat has red collar, laced in yellow, light blue lapels and cuffs, laced in yellow, dark blue cuff-slashes, piped in red, and white turnbacks piped in red. The sword knot is red.

(C) Drummer of Grenadiers of the 33rd Line Regiment, 1807. The shako has red upper band, cords, tassels, pom-pon and plume. The white coat has violet collar, lapels, cuffs, cuff-slashes and turnbacks, all laced in yellow. Yellow chevrons, six per arm, decorate the sleeves. The epaulettes are red.

(D) Drummer of Grenadiers of the 42nd Line Regiment, 1808-1810. He has managed to retain his bearskin cap though it no longer bears the familiar copper embossed plate. The plume is red and the cords and tassels are white. The sky blue coat has yellow collar, lapels and cuffs, all laced in yellow. The cuff-slashes are sky blue with yellow lace, the turnbacks white with yellow lace. The epaulettes are red.

(E) Drummer of Grenadiers of the 27th Line Regiment, 1808-1810. The bearskin has a red plume and white cords and tassels. The dark blue coat has red collar and cuffs, piped in white, orange lapels, piped in red and red turnbacks. The cuff-slashes are dark blue with red piping. Seven chevrons of yellow lace on each sleeve. The epaulettes are scaled with copper, the crescents and fringes are red.

In voltigeur companies, two cornets instead of drummers was the norm;

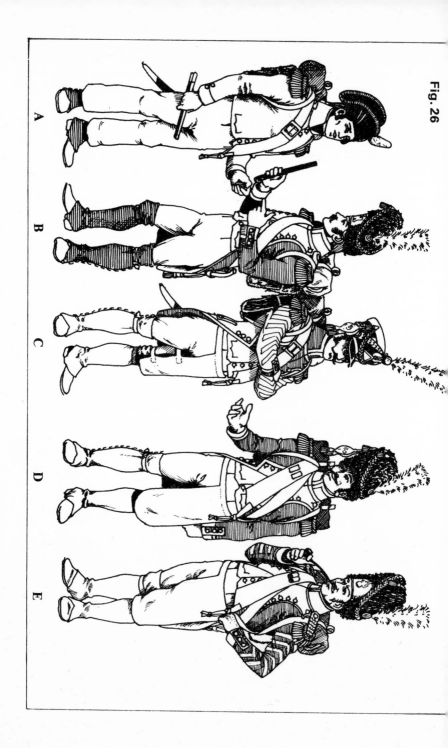

Fig. 26

A

B

C

D

E

however, many regiments, finding one cornet per company sufficient, transformed one into a drummer.

The cornet itself was a total of 2.21 metres long and was twisted into three and a half hoops, the fattest of which was 18cm in circumference. The mouthpiece was 9cm long.

Attached to the cornet was generally a green cord, 2 metres long, with a large tassel at either end, that was passed over the left shoulder. Unlike drummers, cornets carried a musket, the cartridge-pouch of which hung on the same hip as the cornet. Their armament was completed by a short sword and bayonet hung over the right shoulder in the same manner as the men.

Fig. 27 illustrates a few of their colourful uniforms, and gives some idea of their diversity.

(A) Cornet of Voltigeurs of the 18th Line Regiment, 1805-1806. The bicorn has a yellow over green plume and three yellow slashes on each side. The dark blue coat has a yellow collar, laced in yellow, light blue lapels and cuffs, laced in yellow, and white turnbacks with red piping. The cuff-slash is dark blue with red piping. The epaulettes are green with yellow crescents. On the left upper arm we note a single red service stripe. The white sword knot has a yellow tassel and green fringe. The corn has a green cord with yellow tassels and green fringes.

(B) Cornet of Voltigeurs of the 33rd Line Regiment, 1807. The shako has yellow upper band, cords, tassels, pom-pon and plume. The white coat has violet collar, lapels, cuffs, cuff-slashes and turnbacks, all laced with yellow. The epaulettes are also yellow, as are the chevrons of lace on the sleeves. The sword knot and corn cord are yellow.

(C) Drummer of Voltigeurs of the 33rd Line Regiment, 1807. Entirely the same dress as for the preceeding cornet, excepting for the removal of the cords, tassels, and plume.

(D) Cornet of Voltigeurs of the 56th Line Regiment, 1808-1810. The shako has the unusual feature of orange upper band, cords and tassels. The plume is red over yellow and its base is a green pom-pon. The dark blue coat has yellow collar, orange lapels, cuffs, turnbacks and cuff-slashes. This last is piped in white; all the rest have white lacing. Note the white lace 'tabs' on the lapel buttons. The epaulettes are entirely green.

(E) Cornet of Voltigeurs of the 18th Line Regiment, 1808-1810. We return to the 18th to find a considerable difference has taken place in the cornet's dress. The shako is adorned with green cords and tassels, a yellow, over red, plume tops a yellow pom-pon. The dark blue coat has yellow collar, crimson lapels and cuffs, and white turnbacks. The lace about all of these is the tri-colour type illustrated in colour with the livery. The cuff-slashes are dark blue, edged in the same lace. The epaulettes are green with yellow crescents. The sword knot is yellow, the cornet cord green.

The 1812 regulations specified a new green coat for all musicians. Equipment remained largely the same and headgear followed that of the men. Details of the Imperial Livery are given with the colour plate on page 28.

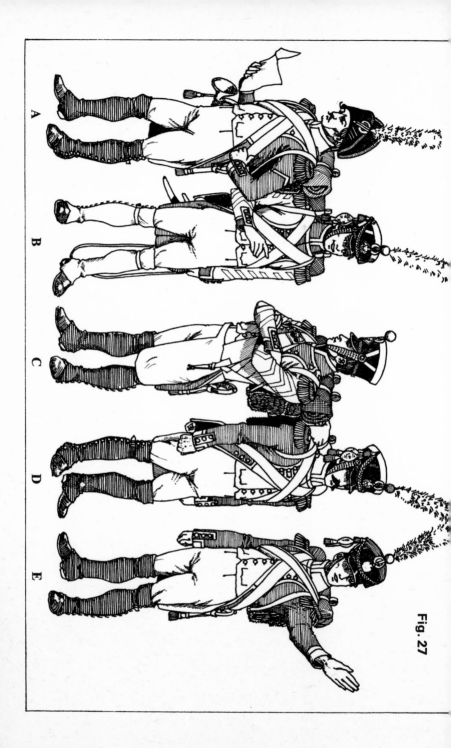

Fig. 27